SYLVIA'S FARM

Published by Bloomsbury, New York and London
Distributed to the trade by Holtzbrinck Publishers

All papers used by Bloomsbury are natural, recyclable
products made from wood grown in well-managed forests.
The manufacturing processes conform to the environmental
regulations of the country of origin.

Library of Congress Cataloging-in-Publication Data

Jorrín, Sylvia.
Sylvia's farm : the journal of an improbable shepherd / Sylvia Jorrín.
p. cm.
ISBN 1-58234-401-9 (hardcover)
1. Jorrín, Sylvia. 2. Shepherds – New York – Catskill Mountains Region –
Biography. 3. Women shepherds – New York – Catskill Mountains Region
– Biography. 4. Farm life – New York – Catskill Mountains Region.
I. Title.

SF375.32.J67A3 2004
636.3'01'092 – dc22
2004000845

First U.S. Edition 2004

1 3 5 7 9 10 8 6 4 2

Typeset by Hewer Text Ltd, Edinburgh
Printed in the United States of America by
R.R. Donnelley & Sons, Harrisonburg, Virginia

SYLVIA'S FARM
THE JOURNAL OF AN
IMPROBABLE SHEPHERD

SYLVIA JORRÍN

BLOOMSBURY

This book is dedicated to Liz Gruen Rose who opened the first page, to David Dalton who continued the second, and my dearest brother Arnold Brickman who has always been there for me.

A special thanks to Ernest Westcott and his blue pickup, who saw to it I got where I needed to go.

CONTENTS

CONTENTS

PREFACE

I SAW THE house, last night, as it was the first time I came upon it, rising suddenly to view tucked deep within a valley, high in the foothills of the Catskill Mountains. It took my breath away then as now. Surrounded by white snow and dark green pines, it is a mansion of a certain size, complete with gables and a large bay window rising out of the third floor, equipped with porches and floor-to-ceiling windows and their many small panes of glass. In the moonlight, snow everywhere, covering its roofs, and the edges blurred, it was much as it was when I came to see it, with only a few minutes to linger, the day I had bought it more than twenty years ago.

The house is a Connecticut River Valley shingle-style house, gray and white, very much like the houses of my New England childhood. Its presence is a mystery here in the Catskills. Only the name of the original owner is known, Greenleaf, after whom I named the house. More than a hundred years old, it was in its day the most modern and civilized of houses. "*Fine* 1885" is written on the most remote gable on its north side. With twenty-four rooms, or twenty-five depending on one's count, it has sixty windows, to which I have already added two, and eight exterior doors. I live here, alone, accompanied by a hundred and fifteen sheep, their assorted hundred and fifty lambs (the full contingent only in winter), two cows, their calves, a flock of Toulouse geese, chickens, several Tamworth pigs, two Border Collies, and two marmalade barn cats, all housed in their respective buildings, of course.

I had never intended to become a farmer. My dear grandfather farmed dairy on the Connecticut shore. My grandmother was a lady, who spoke French with a perfect accent and had a maid to brush her hair before she married her handsome beloved. She never allowed any of her five daughters to milk. She was afraid their hands would become coarse, and they would not find city husbands. Oh, were you to see my hands today, what would you say to me? My poor farmer grandfather had only two sons, his firstborn who was never destined to milk, and his last, who hauled milk cans in a horse-driven wagon to sell to the neighbors on Society Road in Niantic, Connecticut.

I remember the farm as if it were yesterday. The 1790s house, with four fireplaces stemming from one central chimney, still stands. The land has long been divided, but the barn remains, as do the apple trees under which my mother was married seventy-five years ago. My great-grandparents lived on the flat top of a hill in the middle of an orchard overlooking the farm. They gave me my first and middle names, those two whom I have never known, as well as a past and part of a future that they could never have imagined. Whenever I climb the hill behind my barn and look off for miles to a mountain two villages away, I think of them. And when I bring my own grandson to the hilltop, I tell him about his great-great-great-grandparents and tell him to tell his children and grandchildren, when this becomes his, about us all.

I had been raised to fear animals of all shapes and sizes regardless of domesticity. It was easiest for my mother to follow her mother's way and dismiss the entire animal kingdom than distinguish between those wild and those domestic. And so when I first bought Greenleaf, it was with amazement that I heard her say, "You must have a dog, you need a dog, you must promise me you won't go into the woods without a dog." Owning a dog seemed to be an impossible feat at the time. I went into the woods anyway. Alone.

The first years here were spent on restoring the house to its former glory, or rather trying to restore it to its former glory. It had been left empty for seven years before I saw it and asked the realtor (exhausted from driving me around the country looking for the perfect house) to back up the car. "The house we just drove by. I'll take it. Find me the owner. That's the house I want." I bought it. Three buildings came with it, as well as eighty-five acres of property. Inch by inch I devoted myself to bringing life back into the house and land.

When I first set foot in Greenleaf, I knew I could never be depressed living there. Afraid, perhaps; overwhelmed, possibly; frustrated, no doubt; but never depressed. The house has its own life, its own quality, which dominates over all else. It delights. It delights all who enter it. And it still has the capacity to delight me.

When friends would ask what I was going to do with all that land, it is fifteen city blocks long and a quarter of a mile wide, and pressed on to ask if I would keep animals in the great old barn, I'd say, "no. I can't imagine raising animals. I am afraid of dogs, and cows terrify me." Raising sheep had never occurred to me.

One day, when the circumstances surrounding my life were about to come together in a cacophony of disasters and epiphanies which were changing my life forever, I was on my hands and knees, intensely working in the perennial border. John Firment, the man who had once owned Greenleaf, stopped by. He asked me to take a walk with him across the road to look at the boundaries of the property that had once belonged to Greenleaf and still belonged to him. "I know you were always interested in those boundaries," he said. I never was, but knowing he had a compelling reason to take me with him, I went.

A farm truck had stopped on the road, yellow, rusty, and battered, two tires resting on my front lawn. Two men climbed out and took fence posts, drivers, nails, and hammers out of the truck. They each wore winter hats, that beautiful May afternoon, earflaps moving as they walked, tie strings trailing in the breeze. One of the men was of medium height, thin, bearded, slight of build. The other was larger, sturdy, much bigger in form and stature. He didn't have a beard but looked as if he were considering one. I watched them from a vantage point on top of a stone wall on John's property. The two men barely spoke to one another. But they worked as if two halves of the same intent. It was a ballet without music that was being performed in front of my eyes. May skies. Thorn apple in bloom, its scent filling the air. There was neither a superfluous motion nor a movement without grace. They were laying up boundary lines by building fence. John wanted me with him as a witness. No boundary lines altered there. I knew he had a motive beyond my supposed interest. They finished. We all went down to the road. The smaller of the two men climbed into the driver's seat from the roadside. The larger had to cross my lawn in order to climb into his side of the truck. We both knew that entitled me to speak to him. "Do you ever work for anybody else," I asked. He said something that made me think that he may have said "maybe."

I asked him if he were interested in working for me. His head still down, he slammed the door to the truck and repeated the same sound that gave me the impression he had said maybe once more. And that was the first moment of the creation of this farm.

One afternoon the man in the hunting cap appeared in my backyard. "You wanted me to work. I'll be here tomorrow after milking." I could hardly understand his accent. I never did understand but part of what he said. Gradually he spent more and more of his time working for me on the house. One day he suggested that I raise sheep here. I protested as I always did whenever the subject of

4

raising livestock was presented to me. He then suggested that we create a farm together. We talked about it for four months. We seemed to understand one another. I said yes.

The South Central New York Resource and Development Center gave the farm a fine deal on a flock of sheep. They offered nine sheep and the advice of a livestock specialist. Free. A year after the sheep lambed, we were required to return three good ewe lambs a year to the program until the nine were replaced. In turn, they would pass those sheep on to another new shepherd.

That year they presented a choice. As our farm was the last to apply for a flock, they would give us, immediately, a flock of nine very miscellaneous sheep. Should we refuse, we would have to wait for the last flock of the year to be distributed. Should there be more applicants than available ewes, it might mean a wait for another whole year. We chose to begin immediately and accepted the nine miscellaneous ewes.

And so one day, a small pickup truck pulled into the driveway at Greenleaf. Phil Commings, the grand gentleman of sheep farming and the livestock specialist from the R&DC, was driving. His wife, Pauline, was by his side. Phil opened the gate of the cab. Out came a huge black ewe with a classic Suffolk head, to be named Ophelia. Then came a short, chunky gray ewe with a squat Southdown body, to become Amelia. Lavinia Brandon and Lady Fettiplace, two Finn-Landrace sheep, followed. Megan and Brigit, two Dorsets; Collette du Bac, a huge Corriedale, and a huge low-slung crossbreed who became Miss Pettitgill came next. One Southdown ewe, whose name escapes me, followed. Then, staggering on sticklike legs, thin enough to be nearly transparent, came an old Finn-Landrace sheep, mother to Lady Fettiplace and Lavina Brandon. "She's free," Commings said. "If you don't want her, I'll take her back." I knew back meant the dog food factory. "I'll take her," I replied.

5

And so arrived Penelope, the mother, grandmother, and great-grandmother of most of my ewes. A fine sheep she was. Renowned, still. My daughter had come to celebrate the first arrival with us. And the man who said maybe and whose idea it all was, was here as well.

I made a noontime farmer's dinner, served on my best dishes. White linen tablecloths, starched and ironed, were on the kitchen table. We bowed our heads and said grace. The farm, which had begun as the dream of a man wearing a woolen hunter's cap with the earflaps down one May day, became, a year later, a reality, with nine miscellaneous sheep running around the barnyard, pasture, meadow, and the neighbor's front lawn. And with the man, no longer wearing the cap, and me as their shepherds. The sheep were wild. They were from different flocks and therefore didn't know one another. They made a practice of knocking me over, or trying to on a regular basis. When penned in the barn they raced in a broad circle, challenging me to catch them if I could. Feet needed checking; gums as well. Ear tags were wanting to be inserted. There are many reasons why sheep need to be caught and examined. They knew them all and also understood I didn't know how to catch them. I'm convinced that they knew precisely what they were doing in those days, the days that seem so long ago.

Gradually, the farmer's granddaughter who knew nothing of farming became, in the deepest sense of the word, a farmer herself. Imperceptibly, slowly, the mind began to become still. The eye began to perceive and the ear achieved its voice. They shall teach you what you need to know to take care of them, I was told in the beginning. I had dismissed the notion as both too impractical and too esoteric. The fence builder who became my business partner had several conditions to which I must agree, however, should I accept his proposal to start a sheep farm. The first was "no books," or I'd "get ideas which would make more work" for him. I said yes to that one. Listening to what the sheep had to tell me was to be the only way by which I could learn to take care of them. The other was that I wasn't under any circumstance to go near the sheep because they may knock me down. He built me a bench. I painted it a pale peach color. He placed it on a lawn overlooking the barnyard and said, "You can sit here if you want to but you can't go any closer." I said I would. I lied and he knew it.

Every morning I'd get up shortly before dawn and make my coffee. I'd then pull on a sweater, Catskill summer morning, and go down to the barn where the sheep had spent the night. The floor had been limed and a little spoiled hay strewn around. I'd sit on the sill of the barn and watch the sheep in wonderment. Restlessness possessed me. I wanted so badly to know, to know everything. To already be what even at that moment I was becoming. I wanted to have happened what was in the process of happening. At first, the sheep delighted in running away from me. While in the barn they'd stand in a corner as far from me as possible and stare. When I'd open the door, they'd break free, as one, and then scatter. Donald had installed barbed-wire fence intending to enclose them in one section of the farm, but he was a dairyman and fences are different for cows. Sheep have fleeces; therefore, barbed wire means nothing to them.

He farmed dairy with his father and brother on the family farm down the road and was used to working for wages, both on the home farm and for the neighbors on his days off. He was not used to working for himself without wages. He never had. It became quickly apparent to him that if he put up fence on our farming venture, there was no cash in hand at the end of the day. If he built a porch for me, however, or laid a stone floor in my outdoor living room, there'd be money when the job was finished. And so the fence was built, sparely, and my wood room floor beautifully laid with stone.

Tension and confusion were created. He became tense, I,

confused. The farm was his idea, hardly mine. I knew he'd be subject to relentless teasing about starting a farm with me. A woman and an outsider. When I told him that I knew he'd be teased, he said, "It don't bother me none." He was a direct man, of sorts. I believed him. I think he believed himself, too.

His grandfather on his mother's side was a famous shepherd. In the great days of the railroad, the countryside was laced with accessible routes on which to ship livestock all over the country. They raised more than twenty varieties of purebred sheep and traveled with them to shows up and down the East Coast. They still raise a highly respected flock of Tunis. Donald's father had a commercial flock as well, and so he was raised around sheep since he was a child. But his family "never did much with them," he'd say proudly, as if that were a mark of glory. "The lambs survived anyway." He had a customer base, knowledge, experience, and muscle. I had a barn, land, hayfields and pasture, and a small amount of cash. I had time, a commodity of which he had precious little. His wife had left him somewhere in between the time he first started working for me and his proposal that we start a sheep farm together. She left the children with him as well. His commitment to being a father was a driving force in his life. And it spilled over into his handling of the sheep. Sometimes.

I honored my promise to read no books and spent my mornings in the barn staring at the sheep. There was a hole in my heart when I was with them, an empty place that grew larger as the mystery of them and what I was facing became increasingly evident. Slowly, they became accustomed to me. And gradually, one by one, they would approach, tentatively at first, increasingly trusting. Penelope, my see-through ewe, was the most brave. Or wisest. It was she who first allowed herself to be touched and fussed over. Every night I'd try to put them into the barn. At first it took more than an hour every evening. But gradually they began to come in more easily. "Come on," I'd call. "Come on."

One day the sheep were to be brought to the barn for an inspection. We were in the R&DC sheep program and Phil Commings was committed to regular visits. Donald came with his two sons to gather in the flock. Arms flailed. Voices barked commands. The nine sheep were on the run. The boys drove them into the cow path. The sheep broke and leaped over the stone walls into the pasture. Gathering, scattering. Again and again. I moved into the cow path and began to call, "Come on. Come on." The sheep headed toward me, a stampede. "Get out of the way! They'll knock you down! They'll jump the wall!" I didn't move. I stood absolutely still and called, "Come on, come on." And they did come to me, swerved, raced past me, and ran into the barn. I laughed. Donald scowled. His sons slapped each other on their shoulders and began to laugh and tease their dad.

The sheep now come to me whenever I call, "Come on, come on." Almost always. "Come on" has become, "Cahm ahn, cahm ahn." Yankee for "come on." I've added commands that I know the sheep all understand. "Don't knock me down. I'm all you've got." "You're very bad girls." "You're very good girls." "Go." "Steele, put them in the barn." "Enough." "No good." And "steady." Many know their names. They know when we are visited by friends and when we are visited by customers who shall take their lambs. They know when they can get away with mischief and when they can't. They know when they need me and when they don't. But "Come on" was the first command they, as a flock, understood.

Donald and I had gone to the County Clerk's office in the Norman Rockwell Town Square in Delhi, New York, the county seat, and signed the documents making us legal partners in the sheep business. We were both proud of doing it that way. It made it seem both more serious and more lighthearted. No one but us believed the partnership would last. They were all correct. We were wrong. By November I was told the partnership had come to an end. I very much wanted the tension to end, but I didn't want to end the partnership. He had a different point of view.

Suddenly I was facing the first winter alone with the sheep. I was terrified. I had honored my agreement not to read anything about sheep and was, therefore, in total ignorance. By that point there were eighteen ewes and a particularly violent ram on the farm. The ram hated me. The ewes were uncertain. There was no glass in many of the barn windows. No doors that shut properly. No electricity and no running water. I was both out of work and out of money. December came in with a ferocity that has not been equaled since. There was not a day that the thermometer registered above zero. The weathermen said it was the coldest December in recorded history. I borrowed *Raising Sheep the Modern Way* from the public library, bought some extra flashlight batteries, and found a wooden chair on which to sit in the milk house of the barn. I stacked hay against the cracks of the doors, put plastic on the windows, and installed the ewes, minus the aggressive ram. I had no idea when any of the sheep were bred or when any would freshen. Some were huge. Some were not. Nor did I have any idea of what to do should the event happen. I propped up two flashlights on the milk house pipes and read the book, over and over again, and looked for signs that the sheep were going into labor. When I became too cold I'd run to the house for a while. And then go back down to sit on that chair, staring at the sheep.

One ewe, Miss Pettigill, was so big she could hardly breathe. I'd sit on the steps of the milk house and let her put her head on my knee. It stretched her body out enough to give her lungs a bit more room. When she freshened, she forgot all about what a kind friend I had been. She decided immediately after her first lamb was born that I was the enemy, again, and ran from it and me until she had to lie down and deliver a second one and, shortly after, a third. She wanted to have nothing to do with them, or me, and ran wildly about the milk house. The floor had been strewn with lime, some straw, sheep droppings, urine, a lot of amniotic fluid, and three slimy placentas. In other words, an incredibly perfect place to begin to learn about lambing. The lambs sensed their dam's panic and ran. So did she. I grabbed Miss Pettigill by the leg and held on for dear life. She dragged me across the floor. She landed on her back. I landed on mine, but I hung on. She lay still, trapped between the wall and me. I stretched my free arm as far as possible, trying to grab one of the little lambs as it raced around the lambing room. They were in a panic. So was I. I lay absolutely flat and grabbed, caught one, slid on my back to the ewe onto whose foot I was still hanging, and stuck the little lamb onto his mother. He nursed. Thank God.

This is the story of the life here, written as it is being lived. It is about the rhythm of the days and their attendant nights, the flow of the seasons and their gifts of joy and sorrow. Above all, it is the story of all of us, my flock, my beloved dogs, the marmalade barn cats, the cows, goats, chickens, geese, pigs, and Giuseppe Nunzio Patrick MacGuire, the donkey. We have together created something far more than any of us could alone. This is our story.

JUNE GRASS ROSE

A FIELD IS coming back, the southeast corner, bordered by the brook and the cow path. It was my worst. The first year I had sheep, I put them on it to graze, goldenrod- and weed-filled as it was. The second year, the goldenrod and weeds were gone, having been chomped and stamped to death by the small flock of somewhat wild sheep. Instead was June grass, quite uniform and consistent, delicate, pale green at first, changing as the summer wore on to an airy delicate shade of rose, exquisite in the evening light. Underneath was beautiful green moss, and everywhere, spindly strawberry plants, bearing neither blossoms nor fruit. Needless to say, the June grass so pleasing to the eye while on an evening walk, was highly unpalatable to the sheep, hard stems and nose-tickling tops, at that. The sheep didn't eat it, leaving that pasture as a last resort for the lazy days when they didn't want to go too far from the barn. Gradually, white clover, the blessing of Delaware County, took over the adjacent field below the barn. Bit by bit the white clover inched forward to invade the field of June grass, grateful that the sheep removed the taller plants and weeds that shaded it from the sun. Please forgive me, June grass. I'm quickly reminded that my neighbor, Ellen Sanford, told me her father made very good hay from it, because, of course, he knew the exact moment when to cut it. But I don't make hay, and you're just not right for summer grazing for sheep. This year, however, I've found the flock grazing that field more often. Mark Clark helped me and my son, Joachim, clean the barn this year with his efficient little loader. He moved one load to my three wheel-barrows full of black gold to the fields. He spread manure where I couldn't have. A third of my barn's output went onto that field. I then spread the piles with a fork. It covered only a modest area, but it is progress.

This morning I put on a jacket over my flannel shirt, Delaware County summer, and went out to see where the sheep were grazing, and to determine if they were to be moved. They were in the field of June grass, but was it quite June grass? Here and there were timothy, and daisies, and large pads of clover, white, and some dots of red, and sorrel, and mallow in bloom, and even some orchard grass. And there around the piles of bleached straw and the places where they were spread was green. Deep, dark, rich, thick green grass. The sheep are bringing the pasture back.

I buy hay. From friends and neighbors, and, one year, Mr. Aitkens. I look longingly at the one last hayfield I've got left as it stands going to waste. It has not been possible to have it cut these past few years, but I always hope. I've been watching hay wagons being hauled up and down the road and having occasion to ride about evenings along the back roads have looked wistfully at the round bales dotting the hills and the square ones through opened doors of partially filled barns.

Of the two most exciting days of the year on my farm, one is the day when the first hay wagon is pulled up to my barn and is unloaded into the mow. Feelings of jubilation, gratitude, and humility always fill my heart on that day. I always want to do something special for the people bringing it, but harvest dinners don't happen anymore. My dear friend Charlotte Kathmann told me about her neighbors cutting corn together, farm to farm, when she was a girl. The women and girls would get together and cook dinner for the noon meal for the men who worked in the fields. It sounded like so much fun.

I buy hay now from a well-respected farmer two or three hills from here. But yesterday, a neighbor drove in and asked me if I wanted some hay his son had just cut. It would be ready to bale tomorrow. The price and terms of payment were both fair and kind. I still would need a great deal more bales for my flock's winter needs, but this would be hay in the barn. I said yes. I'd been cleaning and arranging the top level of the barn all day. It needed only a few hours to finish and to create order out of some bedding I'd bought. "You've made my day," I said.

And so the wagons being hauled up the road today will pull off into my driveway and up the bridgeway into my barn. I won't be making a haying dinner, not this year, anyway. But I will give my neighbor some flowers for his wife, a loaf of bread each for him and his son, some cash, and offer a prayer of gratitude to Him who made all things grow.

PASTEL COUNTRY

W E H A V E been living in pastel country for nearly two months. It started with a pale blue sky outlined in December's delicate gray trees, and the flat planes of white snow. By January the gray and black outlines changed. Suddenly, its onset imperceptible, the hills became a deep rich rose the moment the sun began to set. Stark white, still pristine, rose-colored hillsides, and the sky in varying shades of blue. One afternoon last week the western sky was lined with blue and white stripes, as clearly defined as one of the woolly blankets we're all covering ourselves with in winter. The blue was sharp and brilliant, with a faint wash of green.

Greenleaf is set in Elk Creek Valley. Although it is deep in the mountains, it is bordered by hills on two parallel sides. I have almost never seen a sunset here, at least not the involving kind of sunset I grew up with on the Connecticut shore. So you can imagine the joy I felt knocking on my tenant's door to tell her that, apparently in the way of welcome for her friend here on his first visit, we were indeed having a sunset. Spokes of rose in all shades broke out from a central hub at the sky's edge, filling almost half the sky with color. The snow assumed a faint pink cast, and the sheep outside in the snow became tinted a pale rose as well.

It is February now. A couple of days ago the cocoa brown branches and twigs of the willows bordering my property assumed a faint shade of green. There is a ewe in the barn whose life is leaving her slowly. She went down some weeks ago, still carrying lambs, I

15

thought. There have been sheep in suffering who told me with their eyes to shoot them. This isn't one of them. When fed and watered she looks content, surrounded by everyone else's lambs. The look in her eyes says, "Water me, grain me, wrap me with bedding. I'm cold. But never shoot me. Not yet, anyway." There was a casualty among the twins she had last March. The ram lamb died. The ewe lamb lived. She and her mother became Siamese twins. They moved as one. The lamb ran from me, always hiding behind her mother. It broke my heart. She was ever aware of my presence in the barn and pasture.

One day, after I had long given up trying to tame her, the ewe lamb walked up to me and rubbed her face against me. She was asking to be petted. After I did, she began to spend less and less time with her mother. She now rarely lets me enter the barn without coming over to be admired and petted. What a lovely gift you've given me, my good old friend.

One night, a week or two ago, I noticed my sick old girl was bagging. The next day, having spent too long in the house trying to get the fire going, I climbed down the ladder once more into the barn. She had just freshened. Her contractions had forced her backward, wedging her into a corner. The lambs were dead.

The water to the barn has frozen. Water has always been the single most relentless source of discouragement in the barn. Each winter season brought some thin strand of hope, only to break into tiny fragments on the ice or snow or stone steps to the barn. Even a plan formed with energy and ingenuity gained only a few days of respite before failing. I carried water, each day, getting wet as the sheep struggled with me, vying for position, to be first to drink. As winter wore on, the prospect of getting soaking wet in the cold became more and more disheartening, and I'd bring down the water closer and closer to nightfall.

The day after the first time the water froze, it suddenly thawed. The sheep, the rafters in the barn, and the neighbors, I'm sure, all heard my voice singing the first two lines of the Doxology, sung from the deepest regions of my lungs and my heart. There was no sound yesterday from the hydrant as I counted to three, the time it takes for the water to come both down from the well and up from the "frost-free hydrant." I carried water from the house to Lady Fettiplace and Olivia and Alice in their respective jugs with their respective lambs, left the door open for the rest to find the snow, and left for my off-the-farm job.

Despair is a luxury I can no longer afford. And I cannot allow so much as a twinge of discouragement to enter my heart. Not this week, at least. I must take a lesson from the sheep looking up at me at the foot of the barn ladder. She's not ready to give up. I'm not, either. I think I may be able to adjust the well to restore the water when I get home, but that won't be for hours. Thank God for the snow.

The joy in the barn is in the form of a little black ewe lamb that has a white stripe down her nose and a couple more on her ears. She's been named after her mother Ophelia Too Applebasher, Ophelia Applebasher for short.

Ophelia is my largest sheep. Chocolate brown, with the most flawlessly beautiful profile of any sheep I've ever owned. She freshens too fast, triplets three out of four times, and has neither mother nor sisters in the barn to help, so if I'm not there when she freshens and the day is cold, her lambs are at risk. My timing was off by five minutes this year. All of my efforts to revive the last of the triplets failed. The second one managed to nurse with a little encouragement from his shepherd. His temperature rose rapidly when I put him and his older sister into a lambing jug. She, the firstborn lamb, pretty little Ophelia Applebasher, already had a round full tummy when I arrived.

My daughter, Justina, anticipating the eventuality of a new metal roof going on the barn, sent me a color card of industrial paints. I dream of the willow green that is the color of some of the farm gates. It will be a subtle contrast of similar tone to the buffs and browns of the hillside pasture beyond it, the rose of the woods in early spring and late fall, the pale green of early summer, and the gray stone walls. It will match for one brief week in April the pastel line of willows bordering the brook beyond the creek. The ever-present snow is still beautiful to my eye. The delicate colors of winter remain pleasing. I'm powdering the top of my freshly baked Shaker Daily Loaf with flour, the white mountain loaf of my childhood. I've just realized what a white mountain loaf is. Now that I'm surrounded by them, I enjoy the one sitting on the blue and white plate on the table even more.

RACING FOR THE GOLD

H ARRY GRACEY shot Lavinia Brandon the other morning in the barn. Lavinia, my oldest ewe, had been down for some time but mothering everyone else's lambs from her ensconced position in the lamb creep, quite unwilling to die. The morning before, I had gone down the ladder to the sheep level of the barn. Lavinia's alert and expectant face was not looking up at me. Instead, she was lying on her side, struggling and thrashing in a futile attempt to stand.

I turned her over and straightened her out. Blood was oozing down her face from a cut over her eye. I cleaned her up and fed her, but Lavinia was no longer the same. The next morning I found her wedged into the spot in which she had so long lain, her legs raw and bleeding from flailing about. Her eyes had lost the alert, eager, intelligent look I was so accustomed to seeing. They now expressed absolute agony. The moment had arrived.

I called Robbie Kathmann, a dairy farmer down the road, who suggested that Harry Gracey might help me, and he so kindly did. I fed Lavinia one last bowl of lamb milk replacer—a mixture diluted with water and a shot of molasses is what had kept her going since she went down. Harry and I lifted her to a corner in the sun away from the others, and he shot her. Mercifully.

There are now four left of that miscellaneous group of sheep, my starter flock Phil Commings drove in with that beautiful day nearly five years ago. Of my original girls, only Lady Fettiplace, Ophelia,

Collette du Bac, and Amelia Simpson remain. They had ten lambs between them this year. Collette's twins died due to a misadventure. Lady Fettiplace's little ram, Sir Pegasus, will stay on to breed young stock. His sister shall stay as well. Ophelia's little black ewe, Ophelia Applebasher, and Amelia's little ewe, yet unnamed, shall stay. Sentiment compromises wisdom in my choices regarding these four.

I'm not certain what it is that I hate most about being a shepherd. Is it when I am the direct cause of the killing, as in the case of Lavinia, or the indirect cause, as in the instance of a newborn lamb freezing to death because I lingered ten minutes too long over the morning's coffee and its mother made an unfortunate choice in the dark, vacant, windy corner in which she freshened? Perhaps the worst is when I see my lambs trussed and chucked into the boot of a car or the back of a van, or maybe it is that horrible feeling that never leaves, going to the barn, six, seven, eight times a day and dreading that slow, searching walk around the perimeter, peering into the corners to see if death had climbed down the ladder before me. Sometimes it still feels too hard a thing to do to put that foot on the top rung and climb down.

My job is a paradoxical one. Keep everyone alive, safe, and healthy in order to kill them. Some of them. Some shepherds resolve the moral and philosophical dilemma. I'm one of those who haven't. I live within the order of things. My task is to maintain my position on the side of life and fight to keep it, and within that I must accept the ultimate order of death.

This morning the sun hadn't stepped over the line of hills in the east when I started for the barn. The day had begun by being bitterly cold. The house had arrived at a record low temperature indoors, and my bedroom was a startling ten degrees when I awoke. Snow drifted two feet over the path, plowed clean yesterday. I was moving in a reluctant slow motion when I got up. I had a choice. Put on barn clothes to feed the hay and risk my ride to work coming before I'd have time to change, doomed once more to go to my other job in my torn, faded black jumpsuit, or wear a skirt and tights and a good sweater and just throw on a jacket over it. It's discouraging to stumble into work with apologies on my lips for what I look like, albeit an honest representation of what I am, in heart, soul, and body, a sheep farmer. So I put on the skirt.

The day was flawlessly beautiful, winter at its most refined, pale, delicate, and brilliant. The sky was a fragile blue waiting to be broken by the sun still not quite over the hill. If I run fast enough, I thought, I'll be there the moment it rises and fills the barn with light. A newly delivered load of hay blocked the door. I scrambled over the precariously thrown bales, a thin coating of snow making it all a touch slippery. The mow was a dangerous tumble below me on one side. Down the ladder I went, taking a quick look into all the corners, listening as well for that little tin sound signaling a newborn. All the while searching out the presence of death.

My flock lay peacefully on the warm pack on the floor, chewing their cud and watching me. Their lambs were lying next to their mothers or in their own tiny flock, a pile of peacefully sleeping young, together in the warmest spot.

The people door within the barn door was open facing east. I leaned against it. Some sheep stood up slowly, their eyes not leaving my face. Everyone was secure that in due time hay would fill the mangers. No need to remind her to give us our breakfast, she'll feed us shortly. I waited a moment or two. I had made it, just in time. The sun crested the hill and filled the barn once more with gold. The wall, the pack on the floor, the sheep were all the color of gold. The sheep forgave my tears.

DANDELION GREEN

PETERMAN'S CATALOG arrived just yesterday, on the edge of our spring. The first daffodils are in bloom in the front of the house. Late even for us and much welcomed. The ruffled dahlialike version was transplanted from an abandoned garden when I first arrived. I felt both the savior and the thief when I took them. I am glad now. I watched that doomed garden grow and bloom, daylilies between brambles, centura between stepping-stones, a mock orange, once burned to the ground, small twigs emerging. I wheelbarrowed the thinnings and cuttings to my border. The old garden has been bulldozed and is only a memory, but a living reminder continues in my garden. The creek takes turns with itself, overflowing its banks. Every day I clear masses of branches from under the small bridge that spans it. The snow is nearly gone from the hills and from the front lawn. Delaware County spring to me means the drama of water running down the hills through the massive stone wall causing the creek to overflow. It means joy at the sight of spring rains brightening the quick fresh green of April spring runs and embodying a disconcerting mixture of longing and expectation, a wish to hold the moment and extend it, conflicting with the joys still to unfold.

I love the grays of spring skies and the gleaming intensity they give to my favorite shade of willow green. Blue skies have never had the appeal to me in the country that they have for most people. It was only yesterday, while walking the dogs, that I noticed the rushing clouds throughout the pale blue sky reflected in my neighbor's pond, and I realized why. I was raised where blue and green were spotty occurrences, minor interferences between the blue of the New England sky reflected in the broad Thames River emptying into Long Island Sound. Now, that is what makes blue, at best, blue and sea blue green, blue everywhere.

Peterman understands how to appeal to a kind of human longing, in the text for text it certainly is in his catalogs. A wish for something both foreign and familiar, an intimacy with places and things just a little bit out of the ordinary, worlds that exist in imagination far more easily than in reality. He evokes the distinctive longing that accompanies spring, whether of gray or blue sky. We all have experienced it. My neighbor found a newborn lamb in my barn last night while I was at work. Tiny, wet, loud, born to a 14-month-old. She called for instructions. The mother wouldn't nurse it. I told my neighbor what to do. I was so far away. I felt so helpless. Instinct tells me it has only a slim chance of making it. This morning's report, heard while I was still at work, included snow. On the daffodils. The lamb's struggle seems entwined with this spring's, trying to get a toehold on life.

This winter was not as brutally harsh as the one before, though certainly far more relentless. The sheep and I had begun to forget that grass would ever grow. I'm about to order a book once more from the library. It is called *Food in England*, by a historian named Dorothy Hartley. My daughter-in-law tracked it down for me once, but its price was too dear and I still haven't bought it.

The English cherish a tree we view as a weed, the thorn apple, and one of the things they value it for is the first new green tips of the leaves. They eat them, sometimes rolled up jellyroll fashion with thin slices of bacon in a kind of bread. Supposedly it is a tonic and is looked upon as a wonderful first green thing to eat after the brown and orange of winter-stored vegetables. A kind of restauratif, for lack of a better word, for the winter body, starved for green.

My favorite and much-longed-for early spring food, besides asparagus, is dandelion leaves. Once available, I eat them every day at my noontime dinner, boiled potatoes, bacon cooked till crisp but not hard, taken from the pan then drained somewhat of fat, a clove of garlic, well crushed, two handfuls of washed, chopped dandelion leaves thrown in, wilted. A splash of cider vinegar, bacon returned to heat slightly, and all tossed with the hot boiled potatoes. Suddenly longings cease and all becomes right in the world. I love the morning chores in springtime, tending to the flock trimming feet, mucking out the barn, only to come into the kitchen, warm from the woodstove, potatoes boiling, dandelions washed, all ready to prepare and assemble that familiar salad of the French countryside. In a sense I've created the longing that anticipates spring within my own environment, and its satisfaction as well.

My flock and I are ready, quite ready, for the dandelion greens.

SHEARING PAST,
SHEARING PRESENT/OF COURSE,
YOU SELL THE WOOL

I T I S A N April day this May 17th, damp, raw, and rainy. The colors of the trees are pink and wine and claret and willow green and cream. The kitchen was a startling, but not unexpected, forty-six degrees when I came home early in the afternoon, after bringing my fleeces to the wool pool in Norwich.

I've made coffee and started the fire and eaten some of the strawberries I bought on the way home. Today is a day off for me, of sorts. One of the three I've had this year. I'm reluctant to change into barn clothes; I'd like to hold on to the slightly altered perspective just a little longer.

Today, the annual spring ritual was repeated. Sheep, relieved of their winter coats a couple of weeks ago, spring forth across the brook and up the hill to pasture. And all shepherds embark on what is for most a longish journey to the Collecta. Vans and trucks and pickups all join in the long, slow line to unload bags of fleeces onto a table to be sorted and tossed into great wheeled wooden trolleys, rolled and lifted onto a scale, tipped and dumped onto the floor, pitchforked into piles, and pushed into a press. Which is then hand-cranked to tightly fill the huge burlap bags. Gone are the days when they were packed by people jumping into them. Noticing the repeated glitches in the working of the press made me wonder once more about the true efficacy of some of our labor-saving devices. The long row of coarse bags holding the wool stacked against the wall looked amazingly similar to drawings I've seen in old books.

We all watched the bags being emptied out onto the table. Arthur Hillis did most of the lifting and organizing with a spirit of willingness and cooperation, a very arduous job. We watched and talked some and watched again.

A few years ago, before any idea of owning sheep ever entered my mind, I wrote a research paper about wool. Mediaeval English wool, to be exact. I had both a personal and professional interest in the subject. As I was bent on becoming a mediaeval historian and needed to learn how to research, it was a perfect fit. How perfect, I wasn't to learn for some time. David Bernstein, my history professor at Sarah College, helped me design the research project as part of my conference work in his class.

The Cistercians, in 1131, settled a barren area of Yorkshire laid waste and depopulated some decades earlier by William the Conqueror. The handful of monks brought with them sheep, primarily to shear to produce the wool needed to make the monks' white habits.

I embarked on the task of researching the history of these monks, with specific interest in learning about the development of their use of wool into an industry. Its subsequent renown and amazing impact on England continues today, where the current economy remains substantially buttressed by the sale of wool and clothing made thereof. Never dreaming that I should ever "farm it," ever raise sheep or have fleeces of my own, I started a most delightful and somewhat dusty journey.

The most fun was when I read about the old methods of training one's "dogge," how to shear the sheep, roll fleeces, wash and clean them, obtain lanolin, and skein yarn. Of the sheep, nothing was lost. Of course, this fit perfectly into a corner of my Yankee soul.

Shearing and the handling of wool is not very different today from in the thirteenth and fourteenth centuries. The principal difference seems to be in the shears. Few still clip with the hand shears used for centuries. The biggest change is that we waste more, use less, and work as much. We may even have fewer of the attendant pleasures.

I had expected little from this year's shearing. I was uncertain if the yield would be worth the trucking. Two fleeces were from five-month-old lambs, three were from ewes that had rubbed theirs nearly off, and I held back two from which to make pillows. But the letter from the wool pool was encouraging, and I packed the sixty or so that were left. I must be lifting too many fifty-pound bales of hay to judge how heavy twenty pounds is. The sacks of fleeces all seemed like ten pounds to me. So that yellow slip of paper given to me at the end of the Collecta held a surprise. At first I thought the number representing my earnings was the weight. There must be some mistake. But no. The sheep shall pay for their own shearing this year.

It was a time to smile and strike up conversations with people never encountered before or perhaps seen only once or twice a year. A time to tell the truth or to lie, the truth too disheartening, sharing stories quietly and slowly. The stories all seemed to be infected with a kind of almost imperceptible joy.

There remains a quality about newly shorn wool, however, that defies explanation. And this quality, a kind of very quiet, very basic satisfaction, has a kinship similar but not identical to the sights and smells and pleasures of the bread bakeries that exist in neighborhoods like the Lower East Side of New York and the seventeenth arrondissement in Paris. The customers have an air of subdued expectancy, culminating in an equally subdued but observable satisfaction. They glance at each other from the corner of their eyes, a trace of a smile around the edges; the selection between the breads from the trays and the wire bins assumes a monumental seriousness and importance. And once in a while a pair of customers, coming together, will gleefully say, "Smell the bread! Isn't it wonderful?"

No one was saying, "Isn't this wonderful!" aloud today, but that feeling was in the air. A lot of us had experienced the comment, "Isn't it wonderful! You must sell the wool," from the many people who feel obliged to comment about our occupation, followed, inevitably by the words, "but I couldn't bring myself to sell the lambs for meat." And now here we all were. Shepherds. With our fleeces. All under one roof. Maybe that feeling of joy and hope in the county fair building was contributed to, in part, by all of those little sparks of joy we'd experienced in people's eyes while saying, "Oh, you sell the wool." For, indeed, yes, of course, we sell the wool.

THE FIRST DAY OF SUMMER

I T I S F I F T Y degrees this morning deep in the mountains on this the first day of summer. I slept with extra blankets, but they were not quite warm enough. The wind was blowing fiercely all through the night. I'd half awaken to the sound of it, convinced that it was raining. I'd fall back asleep to the sound of my own voice inside my dreams saying, "I knew it would rain today. No hay."

Hay is being cut today that is earmarked, in all probability, for me. Last winter I bought hay by the week, delivered, on occasion, to my front doorstep. The snow had made it impossible to drive a truck to the barn. The effects of all events here have a tendency to linger. My lawns are still scarred from the plow's valiant attempt to move six-foot drifts, both blown and packed. And the effect of carrying those 150 bales each week on sleds up the hill to the barn has lingered as well. Acceptance has its grim side. Sometimes, the process I've developed in winter of shutting down my thoughts, or not protesting, "just doing it," can be a little unwise.

And so I sit in the kitchen, waiting for the coffee, wearing both a sweater and a jacket, looking out at the sky that is pristine and blue. A breeze blows through a screened-in window, lifting the edges of the white linen tablecloth.

Samantha, my new dog, as contrasted with her mother, Steele, my old dog, both neither quite new nor quite old, is allowed, this morning, a rare time in the house. Steele stays with me, and Sam stays out. Don't ask me why: I've forgotten the rationale. Samantha is thrilled to be in the house and rejoices, as only a six-month-old puppy can, leaping and barking and wiggling all around me. She went right to the stove to see if there were any crumbs left from yesterday's baking. There were. And now there aren't.

I love her very differently from the way I love Steele. Steele was treated, before she came to me, with an odd mixture of severity and love. And it shows. She used to disobey her last master on occasion, and he'd throw his hat into the air, jump up and down, and shout at her. She would then make some very irritating and unfortunate maneuvers.

It has just occurred to me, knowing as I do the intelligence of this fine animal, to wonder, was she attempting to train him? Of course! The rationale was, if you yell at me and never allow me to go into the house in the worst of winter and persist in feeding me generic dog food, I'll sometimes run the sheep (he had four hundred) in the exact direction that you don't want them to go. Until you learn not to yell, stomp your foot, and throw your hat. He didn't. I was more easily trained. Steele came one April day to begin her new life with me. She never looked at the truck when her prior owner drove away.

We went out in the meadow together that first day. I tested her, saying, "Home." She went straight to my back porch and stood at the door. I opened it and in she went.

When Jim, her original owner, came to tea one day several months later, Steele sat on her favorite chair in the living room and watched us. As he left, she turned her head away from the door and seemed to gaze into the farthest distance a dog's mind could imagine.

The first year we were together, Steele occasionally performed the reverse of the maneuver that I needed. I quickly learned that she needed to think she was more important to me than the sheep. I'd then stop everything, go over to her, and make her run through the basic commands. "Come on by" being a left turn, "away to me" a right. "Put them in the barn." "Bring them to me." "Steady." "That will do," which brings her to a stop and then a straight-line run to me. I'd do whatever was required to reinforce our rapport, repeating the necessary move until she was satisfied, perhaps, that I'd never or rarely ever yell at her, never throw anything at her, and always love her. She seemed to have trained me thoroughly, because we haven't gone through this refresher course in some time.

In the winter, Steele sleeps on a washable throw on my bed. In the summer, she sleeps on her favorite chair in the living room. And when guests come, she is in perfect readiness to show her skills in an informal sheep demonstration, rushing to the spot I always put her on to begin the exercise.

We have our routine. I whisper to her, "Come on by, I want those sheep in the barn," as she stands next to me at eager attention. And off she goes. A visitor once asked me, "What did you tell her?" "I told her to make a wide left-hand turn behind the flock and bring them across the brook, over the bridge to the barn." "No," she said, "you couldn't have." "What did you just see her do with those hundred sheep?" I replied.

Steele loves to swim and fish in the little swimming hole we have in the brook. She is alert in motion, especially if one of us is there to throw pebbles for her to try to catch in midair. It is her favorite game, this huntress who tries to catch birds in flight and catches frogs in the culvert in the summers with my grandson. And now she lies on the back porch in the sun as I sit on the grass, seemingly asleep but in fact absolutely alert.

Samantha had quite a different beginning. She was one of six puppies I had no intention of keeping. From the day of her birth, she always distinguished herself from the others by rolling out of the dog bed and away from her brothers and sisters while they slept in a puppy pile on top of one another. She'd insist on sleeping off to one side all alone, and I'd always pick her up and put her back with her mother. When a friend who knows dogs better than anyone I know came to see the litter, it was the little black-faced dog that she thought I should keep. I didn't want a puppy. Protested vehemently. And kept Samantha.

Samantha's nature is different from her mother's. Her upbringing as harsh in its own way because I wouldn't let her in the house. Even after I decided to keep her, she slept on an enclosed porch, never allowed indoors. Sam's nature is sweet, however, and she sits next to me whenever she finds me seated. Now that I've moved outside with my coffee, she is stretched out on a cold stone patio floor wanting so badly to be next to me rather than lying in the sun like her mother. She swims with glee, if a dog could be said to be gleeful, making little happy noises and paddling in the swimming hole while her mother ardently fishes.

I'll soon train her for sheep. Last evening she sat motionless on the stone wall while I visited with my flock. It was the first time a "down stay" command was obeyed with apparent understanding of why it was necessary. She's ready. She flocks her little horned Dorset-Finn cross lamb, Sir Parsley (the origin of his name and why he thinks he's a dog, sleeps with Samantha, and refuses all contact with his own species is another story). She is showing a herding instinct at about the right age.

Steele and Cagney, Samantha's sire, made some beautiful puppies. There were two, though, that broke my heart to let go. Both were prettier than Steele or Samantha, with their mother's brains and their father's handsome elegance. One, I heard from Jake Bryden, who trucks livestock every day up and down these country roads, is already bringing in cows at Liddle's farm in Andes. I had seen him in passing one day, thinking, oh, what a nice dog, before I realized it was he.

I'm sitting in one of the most beautiful spots here at Greenleaf. The morning brings glory to the color of the flowers. There is a stone window in my outdoor living room with a view of the barn and an apple tree and newly framed leafed ash. The willow against the dark gray carriage house gleams in the sun, gold and green. The wind moves the leaves, making it all almost too dazzling to look at. I'd love to photograph that willow, mornings. It is so enchanting with white fog behind it or as now many shades of green. I'd forgotten how much I've loved to sit here. It's been too long.

Steele, Samantha, and I walk each morning to my neighbor Nina Juviler's mailbox and then back home. I'm teaching Sam to heel. She does most times. We look at the progress Henry Kathmann and I have made on my most interesting sheep fence, and at the neighbor's geese, and enjoy being together. It's our time.

COWS

THE RAIN comes, tin sounds on the porch, the buzz and sizzle of cars driving by, a rat-a-tat-tat on the porch roof, a plaintive wail from a drenched lamb looking for her mother. The sounds usually bringing comfort and joy here in the grass crop country somehow today bring despair. Last year's hay was unaffected by the decent snow of the prior winter and very much affected by the drought. I couldn't find hay throughout the summer or fall and was forced into buying hay by the week all winter. This year we have had rain. Days or, rather, nights on end. Major storms accompanied by twisters, tearing branches from maple trees along the creek. Thunderstorms turning the sky slate gray, small steady drizzles. And today's steady rain.

Grass is growing quickly in the fields where growth has been slow. The sheep spend their midday naptime directly behind my barn. The runoff has sweetened the field beyond it, and it has become a dark, rich green. But what it all means is that the hay I customarily buy in June is not in the barn. And the July crop was not dry enough, in my judgment, although dry enough in the seller's.

The week has had some comic relief, however, in one or two forms. I raised a Jersey calf a couple of winters ago, from the time she was a week old. She had been trained to a pail and had her own spot in the barn. When it got cold I put a hooded sweatshirt on her, and once, when she got too cold, Falvius Mauer took her back for a week to his warm and dry cow barn. I bought a beautiful rolled leather halter lead for her and taught her to walk like a lady. And that was part of her name: Lady Francesca Cavendish. She was lovely. My only mistake was in not disbudding the horns. They grew. At first I looked for pictures of Swiss cows with garlands around them. I even found a beautiful picture of a French sheep with an elegant straw headdress. Oh, to know how to braid that!

Lady Francesca lived with the sheep and seemed to think of herself as a sheep, albeit, a gradually bigger and bigger one, but a sheep nonetheless. Then one day my sweet docile calf became a heifer. And as her life changed, so did mine.

The sheep were fence and stone wall climbing in those days over to Tom Connelly's. Lady Francesca, lumbering along, would follow. But sheep could scoot between barbed wire when encouraged back home, and Francesca just couldn't. She finally learned to duck her head between double-strand sections in the fence, but on more than one occasion was left bawling on Connelly's side at the retreating backs of both Steele and me, after I had gone over to retrieve my flock.

One day Francesca discovered the heifers at Connelly's. The A-I man from Eastern had done his job and I thought she was bred. But there was something about the sight of those heifers that drew her like a magnet. Tom drove in, in his Bronco, shouting, "That heifer of yours is going to break down my fence so I put her in with my cows. Get her when you want to." So Steele and I went to Tom's field to retrieve Lady Francesca Cavendish. She took one look at us and ran away. Again and again. Life with cows appealed to her, I presume, and life with sheep did not.

I was suddenly called to New York because of an illness and death of a close friend. It was two weeks before Steele and I were able to return to Tom's field. By then Francesca had become much attached to her new friends and went tearing into the woods at the sight of us.

On the fifth or sixth day, my steps now leaden as I trudged over the rise and up the hill, I found the woods and field empty.

Nowhere was the herd to be seen. Rumor had it that the heifers were sold. Despair filled my heart and failure filled my soul. All dreams for that farmhouse cheddar cheese curing nicely in the cellar and a beautiful new little calf in the fields were gone.

I called Connelly's several times and wrote two letters to him in the fall, realizing full well that I'd probably not reach him. Yet there had to be a way to resolve the issue. I knew he was not a man who could live with his conscience if he profited from the sale of my cow. Connelly is a complex man but has his own sense of justice and his own sense of humor as well. But ultimately he honors his values.

After a few months of thought and procrastination, I made one last attempt. I wrote a final letter describing how Steele and I put his heifers in when they first broke out in the spring. Then, with great care, I broached the subject of Lady Francesca Cavendish. "I know you would be appalled to realize you had profited from the sale of my cow," I wrote.

A few days later, just last week, Tom stopped by the house. "What made you think I sold your cow?" he said. "She is in my backyard."

"You mean she is still alive? I cried for a week when I heard she'd been sold," I said.

Tom danced his Irish jig, or rather I did while he piped for a few minutes. "She's nice," he said.

"I know," I replied. "I trained her to lead."

"What do you want for her?" he said. "You come up and see her."

"No, I couldn't bear it," I replied. "You decide the fair price, I trust you."

"I'll be by in a few days with a check," he said.

The rain seeped into my soul today. The recommendations from the Cooperative Extension yesterday about my fields would be expensive and arduous to comply with. There was nothing I could think of to redeem my day or give any joy to my heart. But then I remembered Tom's visit and suddenly I knew.

I called George Thompson who has a Jersey herd over on Dry Brook. "Do you have a four- or five-day-old calf for sale?" I asked.

"It so happens I do," he said.

"How much?"

"Forty dollars."

"I'll take her," I said.

It was the only thing I could do. And suddenly the rain sounds like music and the cool air inspires me to bake some lemon cookies and brings the thought of having tea when I've eaten all meals walking, between chores, for weeks. And all I can do is smile, and the house feels full of joy.

MY GRANDFATHER,
MY GRANDSON, AND I

M Y BROTHER Arnold, my cousin Henry, and I used to play together summers on Grandpa's farm. We were the youngest of eight children, an oddly small number from my grandparents' seven children. My grandfather and my uncle Percy farmed dairy, milking cows by hand in the gentle rolling hills of Perkin's Corners, Niantic, Connecticut, not far from Long Island Sound. The 1790s house and hundred acres held an infinite source of entertainment for us.

There was a small coppice of a pithy kind of tree on one side of the cemetery wall that bordered the farm. I never did find out what kind of saplings they were. Soft and cocoa colored inside, they invited one's knife to turn them into a whistle.

Sometimes we ran across the beautiful flat top of the wall, laid stone and cement, to get to the little coppice. Other times we skirted the wall and slipped in from the side. It sheltered us and gave us a place for our imaginations to roam, away from our parents, each other's aunts and uncles. I don't remember what our games were exactly about, but do remember the feeling of daring and expectancy upon arriving there, and the shadows, and the tiny flickering of light between the trees high above our heads, and how close we felt to each other, and how special it was to have this place.

One afternoon, crossing back to rejoin the family, I realized that the thick black vine now growing up, across, and down the other side of this massive wall had not been there before. It was a snake. A large one. I was the oldest of the three of us, all of six at the time; my brother and cousin were both four. I was terrified of the snake.

My mother was a farm girl whose mother was a city girl. My beloved grandmother made certain her daughters were raised with the city refinement of being thrown into minor and proper hysterics at the sight of such things as snakes. And so my mother instilled in me a real fear, if not a propensity to have hysteries, of this harmless creature slowly making its way across the wall.

There I was feeling absolutely responsible for my brother and cousin, facing off a very large black snake that was between us and the safety of our parents on the lawn under the trees. "Run!" I shouted to them, and run I did. They followed, two pairs of short little four-year-old legs moving as fast as they could behind me! Breathless, we told the story and were told that of course we should not have strayed to that little wood in the first place.

I'm quite certain that the size of the snake was thought to be exaggerated. It wasn't exaggerated in the least. The last time I turned off the highway onto Society Road, went to the farm, and saw that stone wall, I was as impressed with the size of the wall as I had been that summer day. Somehow, the visits to that wood lost their charm after that afternoon. I had become a bit afraid, and that deterred me rather then enticed me back.

The lay of the land of my grandfather's farm is not dissimilar from mine. The meadowland before the hill was shorter and there was no creek. But the flat top of the hill is the same. My great-grandparents lived up there, in an orchard that they and my grandfather planted. I never saw it. By the time I was born, my mother had become far too much a city girl to climb ever again to the top. I tried, alone, each time going a little higher, each time drawing back when I became enclosed by too many trees.

I know I never saw my grandfather take the dog and rifle and go up into those woods to shoot a fox that had killed some of his chickens, but the story is so vivid in my memory that my imagination has assumed the hue of reality, and I believe in my heart that I did watch him and heard him call, "Nelly, Nelly," and take his beautiful collie and his rifle up that hill and into the woods. I can see his back to me, his head turned slightly over his shoulder, smiling at Nelly, his rifle cradled in his right elbow.

My grandson, Mikhael, has a subscription to the *Delaware County Times* and nearly every week reads about my life on my farm in what he refers to as the news. "I read about it in the news, Grand-mumsiedo," he says. "I read about it in the news!" Will he remember seeing me with my Weatherbee rifle and my dog Steele taking the sheep up the hill to the pasture? Will the stories he's read and the things he's seen blend fact and imagination in his mind about his grandmother, turning me into something a little larger than life, or distilling his memories of me into an essence rather than a diluted everyday self?

I remember my grandfather's bushy mustache, which I encoun-tered when he stretched out his arms and bent down to kiss me, and my mother calling out, "Pa, don't kiss her, you'll scratch her face," and I not wanting to hurt his feelings, running even faster to him, all the while knowing how scratchy that red brush on his face was going to be.

I remember how crystal clear and cold the well water was that came from the pump when he drew me a glass, and how I followed him in the fields while he dug potatoes, picking up the tiny ones left behind, and the starburst of crinkles around his smiling eyes when he showed Arnold and Henry and me the baby chickens in the barn, holding them in his hands.

But what surprises me so is to realize that I am exactly the same person I was when I was a little girl. The memory of the wall and my brother and cousin and the snake exists within me as I am now. It's hard to explain, but the most simple way is to say how surprised I am to realize I was only six on the day of the snake. Grandpa died when I was seven, and the farm was gone shortly after that. I am exactly the same inside, planting potatoes today as I was picking up those tiny ones next to Grandpa when I was six.

My grandson Mikhael is now older than I was when my grandfather died. He visits here less often than I visited the farm, lives here when he does rather than being whisked away in the great black Buick, when Sunday afternoon came to an end. I wonder what of my life here he will incorporate into himself, both memory and myth, and what traces of my grandfather and grandmother and great-grandparents shall remain with him and become alive in him. Will the kind of living memory of Grandpa and Nelly and the gun and the fox and the chickens that I never could have witnessed happening become in Mikhael a memory, reality intermingling with images from the stories I write to create a picture of me and Steele and the Weatherbee and the coyote and the sheep, my back to him, my face to the side, smiling, looking down at the dog, my rifle under my arm, walking up to the hill?

THE MAPLE LEAF

A WEEK OR two ago, while driving along Route 10 in the early morning on my way to the village, I saw a single leaf on a maple tree had turned red. My heart stopped and panic filled my soul. Then just as suddenly, I realized that it was quite premature, for that tree had been slowly dying for quite some time, and it was not inappropriate to have a red leaf or two. I tried to dismiss the dread of an unprepared-for winter from my heart.

My daughter Justine and grandson Mikhael were here for all of last week. For a total of nine wonderful days, Justine and I worked hard on the carriage house and the gardens, organizing Mikhael's room, which had been for too long an ironing and laundry room, painted a great span of picket fence, made nine afternoon teas and nine dinners, twelve loaves of bread, numerous jars of jam, and in general added to the welfare and well-being of Greenleaf and increased the treasure of family memories. Justine did an incredible piece of artwork, enhancing the house. She is a decorative painter by trade and painted a series of leather-bound books appearing as if they were real in a corner of the living room. In other words I was, for a little more than a week, totally distracted from any anticipation of not being ready for winter.

I went to Cooperstown with a friend this week and there they were and it was. "They" were a handful of orange and red leaves on a few maple trees; "it" was another reminder of winter's impending arrival. "The first day of winter is the last day of the county fair" is a common saying here. I'd deliberately avoided knowing the date of the fair. I bought some Christmas presents in Cooperstown. We always shop in advance, so that didn't feel like the onset of winter. Justine stayed an extra day and we picked chokecherries on the Turnpike to make jam but that didn't do it, either. I don't look at calendars and haven't turned the page from July to August yet and am not quite certain of the date. There is about the month of November's worth of wood cut and stacked, and the winter's worth felled but not cut for the hundred-year-old ceramic stove in my room. I've all of the fence posts I need and half of the wood needed to build the latest fence, with half of that assembled and up. Two thirds of the winter's hay is in the barn. The water line is laid, needing amendment but possessing promise. Not much food is put by in the freezer. Three sweaters are knit to wear to the barn, and nearly sewn together.

Sometimes there is unexpected virtue in not having been able to finish something. I haven't had time to address the barn floor since spring. It needs mucking out. Sheep require a pack of straw and rotted manure to keep them warm in winter. I've not let them in the barn except for specific procedures since early spring. Wonder of wonders! The pack has packed. Much less volume and probably much more weight. The big however, is that it means fewer loads of muck to shovel. In some places it is only six inches deep! I had been shoveling some days quite intensely. But this is a bonus. The barn needs a serious uninterrupted day for it to become functional. It also needs the kind of carpentry I can handle myself. For a change. Some things are better here, almost, and only some are worse. The better is far better than ever, and the worse is far worse.

Another set of summer twin lambs was born in the field yesterday, one big, one tiny. It is possible that they started out as triplets and one didn't take early on. Their mother gave me twins in January, little ewe lambs perfect for breeding next summer. I lost a ram lamb, a twin, to hypothermia on the big rain day last week. His momma led us to him huddled next to a stone wall, her lively little ewe hovering beside her. He was alive but just barely. He sounded a heart-wrenching cry that didn't promise much but a frantic effort to save it on my part and usually a hole to be dug. We put him in front of the fire and tried to dry him. I tube-fed him with the most potent mix I could put together, and he died.

Noah Saltonstail's horns are troubling him. I think he may have fly strike. Maxine Brown had success using Pine-Sol in a similar situation. I've seen him several mornings going to rub his head on the cool stones of the barn bridgeway. He must be caught today and treated each day for a while. I need him.

A customer is scheduled to come today to buy a ram lamb, and I shall thereby have money to extend the fence. More to do. I haven't mowed part of the lawn in what seems like forever, and there are the expected loaves of bread to bake to greet my friends and family when they arrive at noon. The floors need mopping and the potatoes need hilling and the garlic is ready to replant and the new gate that was just cut for the new green fence asks to be painted and hung. I haven't even begun to work on the summer's project, promised to myself all winter, to convert the old laundry room, the most beautiful room in the house, into a dining room.

In other words, what shall be completed today, this wonderful one, with fourteen hours still left in it, and what shall spill over into an equally full tomorrow? And what hour, if any, shall be put aside to devote to heeding the message sent to me by that first red leaf on the maple tree one early morning only two weeks ago?

A STORY OF THREE BARNS

S OMETIMES THE most concrete of realities are built from the
most ephemeral of dreams. The massive stone barn at the
Shaker Village in Pittsfield, Massachusetts, the sixty- by thirty-
four-foot rectangular hundred-year-old barn on my farm, and my
grandfather's cow barn in Niantic, Connecticut, are three examples.

I was swept away by the Elk Creek Club this Monday to the
Shaker Village in Massachusetts. Thinking that just outside of Albany
meant a couple of miles on the outskirts of that city, my surprise was
emphatic when Rosemary Sheehan, at the wheel, said, "Oh, Sylvia,
that's Albany," as we swept on past.

My interest in the Shakers is practical. The bread I make in the
summer and early fall is usually Shaker Daily Loaf. It keeps, it is
delicious, and makes the kitchen a joy to enter while it is baking. I've
been putting up all things delicious with tomatoes this weekend and
am making crystallized plum tomatoes today from a Shaker recipe
that has intrigued me for years. But the most important consideration
was to learn what I could from their barns that could possibly help
me in mine.

They have Merino sheep, a breed which I've only seen in pictures.
I had read in Thomas Jefferson's notebooks that he and George
Washington imported several. Merinos remain the worldwide standard as the finest wool producers. The Shakers had been raising
them since the early 1800s. It is a special treat for me to be able to see
them. The Merinos were behind the great stone barn, near to shelter

45

in case it rained. They have deep folds in their necks, which create more fleece and more problems for our contemporary shearer who uses electric clippers rather than traditional shears. The concern about rain stemmed from the sheep having a tendency to develop fly strike because the neck fleeces, once wet, never seem to dry out. The shepherds at the museum hired a man from New Zealand to shear the sheep this year. Since this is the predominant sheep there, he had no problem at all. The characteristic folds in the neck have become systematically eliminated by selective breeding; however, the museum is breeding them back in order to have a representative of the type of sheep the Shakers originally had.

The sheep were a dun color. The rams had fabulous curling horns. The pictures I've seen in advertisements made them seem to be huge animals, fierce and menacing, but those at the museum were Dorset sized. Their snorts and stamping front hooves, lowered heads, and piercing eyes made one certain they are not to be tangled with.

To my disappointment, the building that the Shakers used to house their sheep was no more, and the flock was confined in a conventional setup. But there had to be some solutions to some of my problems here in this barn. And there were, of course. The Shakers had made sturdy shutters to protect the lower two thirds of the windows so the cows wouldn't accidentally kick them in. I've repeatedly put slats over the windows in my ram pen only to have them broken when I first separate him from the ewes. Heavy wooden shutters, high enough to be out of reach of his horns and low enough to allow light in, would do it. It was a good idea, but I continued to look. There had to be something else. Then I found it!

For four years now, I've been making wooden L-shaped brackets on which to hang partitions dividing my barn. The two joinings of the L would separate and come apart. The partitions are critical to the economical use of my barn. They must be high enough so the most energetic of yearlings can't jump them. Sturdy enough so a hungry crew won't gate-crash my heavier diners and I can save on feed, and easy to manipulate. Speed can often be crucial.

Well, there in one building spoking out from the round barn were doorways leading to a two-story drop, protected by a nonhinged sliding gate (hinges are the biggest single expense in my barn). The gates slid into and then dropped in an ingeniously fashioned system cut out of a single piece of wood. The notches held the gates firmly and securely. Beautiful! I saved the price of the ticket on one of those strong hinges alone!

I bought a picture of the inside of the roof of this amazing barn. The rafters are part of a huge wheel forming spokes to the center. In form, it is both elegant and complex. The roof itself is magnificent and modest. I'd love to have been present at the discussion and design meetings that resulted in this building. I wish I could understand the thought processes that originated it.

The first barn I ever went into was my grandfather's. Grandpa used to take me and my brother Arnold and my cousin Henry to see the baby chicks he housed and raised on the upper level.

I remember the warm darkness of this barn, the stars sprinkled across the inside of the roof, round circles of light flashing in dances across the walls and floor, and yet on cloudless days, perfectly still. And then there was the still, thick air and the dust that sparkled in the light, but always the stars, the stars peeping through.

The very first time I walked into my barn, there they were, the familiar sight of stars sparkling in my roof, and sunlight dancing on the walls, and the glistening particles of dust gleaming in the air. How familiar and safe it felt. "Oh, stars," I thought, "this barn has stars in the roof, too."

And now when my boots slosh slosh in the wet after a rain seeping into the stanchion level of my barn floor, and I shoved and put down new hay and lime, I know I have to find the money to put on a new roof, and the stars will then be gone. My heart is heavy at the enormity of the project, and my face becomes grim as I slosh through the waste to get to the shovel. And yet never never has my heart failed to feel that same joy I felt as a little girl when I am in the haymow and see the stars in the roof, stars just like in Grandpa's barn.

TWO STORIES IN ONE:
MY MOTHER'S KITCHEN,
CHRISTMAS 1993

I WALKED DOWNSTAIRS and into the kitchen this morning, the first day of Christmas. It registered a typical forty degrees on the indoor thermometer. Justina and my grandson's mother, Naomi, had created order the evening before, when the intensity of Christmas cooking had reigned. The breakfast table was set perfectly. Blue-and-white dishes on the white linen cloth. Long-stemmed wine-glasses were in place for orange juice. The big white enamel sink was gleaming and empty. The white stove was clean and shiny with blue-and-white dish towels hanging from its handles. My family's boots were lined up near the fire, now down to glowing coals. The white cotton curtains were gathered and pulled to the side to reveal an even whiter world. The sky was white with a faint blue cast, and the massive pines sheltering the house were thick with snow. As I write, the sun breaks through. The pale blue cast to the white sky intensifies, and gold is the snow where grey shadows do not lie.

I savor this moment alone in the kitchen where my family is still asleep upstairs. The ticking of the clock seems especially loud. The kitchen fire has begun to roar, small thunder. Steele has come down from my room to warm herself next to it. Sometimes I come in from the barn and stand on the step leading down into my kitchen, and this room, so central to all our lives, pleases me, its sense of order, its color, its aesthetics. One day last summer, when I had returned from

49

shoveling the barn, I found the room especially comforting. Everything at that moment was in its appointed place. Blue-and-white Royal Copenhagen china lined up against the wall Justina had painted to replicate blue-and-white Portuguese tiles. Her set of blue-and-white ceramic canisters lined up perfectly, their painted windmills pointed all in the same direction on the long shelf close to the ceiling. A bouquet of white mallows was in an equally white pitcher. For a moment I had achieved a feeling in that room that so often eludes me, a feeling both familiar and distant. But what was it? And why was it so deeply satisfying, so urgently important, and so observably missed when absent?

My mother's kitchen on Ocean Avenue in New London, Connecticut and, earlier, on Vauxhall Street in the same town, were very much the opposite of any I've ever created. My mother was not a cook or, at least, not the kind of cook who believes you begin to make a tuna sandwich by catching the fish, and she was certainly never covered with the flour badges I inevitably wear after baking our daily bread. My mother's generation was the first to enjoy canned foods. Foods, that is, that someone else canned, someone else with a name like Del Monte or Ocean Spray. And she certainly enjoyed the advantage of it.

I remember most vividly the kitchen on Ocean Avenue. Gray marbleized Formica on the kitchen table. Black vinyl seats on the chairs. Cream gauze curtains on the windows that shut out neither the summer sunlight nor the dark of winter's evenings. And the pantry where we both spent the evening doing the dishes. I talked and she listened. Everything was in order. There was a place for everything where the everything could always be found. I remember the silence in that room as I rushed into it as a teenager, a whirlwind of joy or despair and everything in between. The silence and security and order. The love in that room was absolute and impenetrable. It almost had to be pushed aside to walk through it. Nothing, nothing could ever cause even a ripple in that silent, thick air. The sense of security was expressed in that order. The knowledge of love was in my mother. And it filled the room in its entirety.

It was that summer morning, standing in the threshold to my kitchen, when I understood the why of it. Why is it so important to me to have that kitchen in order. Why is it so deeply satisfying when it is. My mother's solution to the problem of keeping flower vases clean was not to put flowers in them so they never got dirty. But she always let me fill them, even as a two-year-old, without a hint of reproach. And now, in January, I start to think of forcing thorn apple branches to bloom. And if I don't, a voice inside of me calls out that I am betraying my nature. And yet it's not the flowers alone, nor the order alone, that is satisfying, but the deep, still, impenetrable love and security that they both together evoked that have meaning for me.

My children, grandson, and grandson's mother arrived last week to celebrate Christmas. I have always delighted in the custom of celebrating the Twelve Days of Christmas. It became even more enhanced when I married a man whose culture included a parade on Twelfth Night celebrating the arrival of the Three Kings in Bethlehem. We don't always come together on Twelfth Night, and we don't always finish making our unfinished gifts on Twelfth Night, either, but we believe we do, and we believe we will, and that is our gift to each other in this family, that Christmas isn't one big explosion of giving and one burst of loving one day a year but that our thoughtfulness toward each other and lovingness have no end. There will be a tomorrow, another day to show our love.

Christmas, for us as in many families, is spent with our own particular customs and traditions. When my children were small I had very little money to spare on gifts. But I so wanted to have abundance under the tree that their thrift-shop finery, handmade sweaters, mittens, and long underwear became the gifts. Socks wrapped in individual pairs. Packages of bubble gum. A handmade doll and an apple green car. I remember spending my last dollar on a red Tonka truck that I couldn't bring myself to leave behind for my then three-year-old son. One week we drank only powdered milk because I bought a strand of golden bells for the tree with the last money I had.

Those very bells are on this year's tree, twenty-odd years after I bought them that Christmas Eve. And the socks reappear as well. This year they manifest as gifts from my daughter to my ex-daughter-in-law, peach colored, wrapped beautifully. And from me to my son, once more, black tube socks from Ames, all in a box that had once served quite a different purpose, and handmade ones as well from Micbet's Shearlings. Mikhael was as thrilled with a bottle of pure vanilla extract to use baking chocolate chip cookies with his Daddy-O as he was with still another John Deere tractor added to his collection. Justina took the prize for starting to shop the earliest, last January. Naomi came in second, beginning in May. Jaochim did a most creative Christmas. I, who have been known to do it all in two days before Christmas, was pleased with myself for beginning last summer at the Walton Fair, and even found a forgotten gift of a wooden shoe form left in the back of the Christmas closet.

It took the family five hours to decorate the tree. The ornaments have been gathered since Justina's first Christmas. Painted tin figures from Mexico, a tiny fuzzy brown bear, painted glass fruit, a miniature red sled. The tree was the last one to be found in the village the day before Christmas. And it fit absolutely perfectly in our Christmas tree corner.

I came home from work at nine A.M. on Christmas morning. Gifts were still being wrapped. Everyone helped me with mine. Once or twice they wrapped one for themselves thinking it was for someone else. It took us a day and a half to open them all again. Flashlights and emory boards, Chinese poetry and Emily Dickinson, Bartholemew's atlas, bowl scrapers, and mittens, coffee from Hawaii via New York and coffee from Fortnum and Mason in London, white chocolate with pistachios and dried cranberries, music from the 1930s. Raggedy Ann books, corduroy shirts, beautiful soaps, a rhinestone pin, silk velvet ribbons. Each gift was thoughtfully chosen and given, each an expression of our interest in, knowledge of, and love for each other.

I try very hard to make the moment that my now-adult kids arrive home a step into a house redolent with security, order and, above all, love. I plan and make schedules in fifteen-minute units. What to dust and what to polish and what to bake and when. Sometimes I succeed more than other times. I am, no doubt, forever doomed, or shall I say privileged to have hay from the barn somewhere on the kitchen floor or a motherless lamb under the stove. But always, I try.

As I sit in the kitchen, early this morning, made peaceful and lovely and orderly by Justina and Naomi, a quiet time before everyone comes down, I understand the profound and deep sameness between this pretty, pretty room, smelling of baking and roasting and cooking, and that beige-walled room with black vinyl chairs, and gray Formica table, smelling of Campbell's soup. The love is absolute. Its assumption impenetrable. This room is the same, this first day of Christmas, as my mother's kitchen so long ago.

THE LIGHT in the sky is changing. The afternoons are brighter. Winter is emphatically here. Rarely complimented, much maligned, winter brings within it light and hope. It barely finishes when it hears us say, oh, the dark days of winter. It sends not one extra blast of cold down our chimneys for our misunderstanding. It simply continues, oblivious. It is autumn whose brilliance and fleshy colors delude us into thinking winter's days are dark. Autumn, with its gleaming blue and deep purple skies. Its evenings of opal or hyacinth clouds bordered by russet and gold hills; its mornings, with shining leaves, brilliant in the sunlight. And slowly, slowly, the night grows long and the days short. Darkness thick, sharp, intense, and deep. We watch the brilliant stars. The intensity of color and light has blinded us, enchanted us, and delighted us. And as each day progresses, each one shorter than the one before, we regret the falling of the leaves and the approach of winter's darkness. But it is the day after the first day of winter that brings a half a minute of more light and that gradually leads us in slow increments toward summer.

This winter, each day seems as cold as or colder than the one before. My friend calls to ask, "Have you frozen to death yet?" The water in the house freezes from time to time. Human error (forgetting to leave the water running when it's windy), false economy, my reluctance to run up the electric bill, and not quite being prepared all contribute. I've learned how many blankets and comforters it takes to sleep warmly if I've not the time to stoke the French ceramic stove in my room, and the little dogwood-painted thermometer reads twenty degrees on the cold wall.

I can't remember the principles of heat and cold from high school physics. It would be helpful to understand how heat moves, aside from rising. And is it preferable to put the down comforter as the bottom layer or the top layer on a pile of blankets? Some people like warm climates, consistent, predictable, even temperatures. Others need the changes, the variables of nature. Some move south after living here most of their lives, and some of those return. But those of us who do live here are consistent in our argument that our lengthy mud season, that never-never land between winter and spring, is the most disheartening. That is the time to be prepared for, to arrange special moments of sociability or entertainments of the mind.

There is wisdom in the seed catalog company's decision to send their bright colors into our consciousness a few days after Christmas. I've saved them for the rare times in front of the fireplace in the late afternoon. Shepherd's was especially wise, by design or necessity, to place their bright-colored flowers on a white background on the cover of their catalog. Images of summer juxtaposed on winter's snow. I imagine wine and dark pink roses purchased from Peggy Bolton in Walton planted around my carriage house, and call to order Madam Isaac Perrier, a classically scented rose in dark magenta. A moment for dreams.

When I was a child I spent most of my winter confined to bed and rarely attended school between Thanksgiving and sometime after Valentine's Day. I was passed from one grade to the next because of a combination of a formidable mother and high scores on final exams. I made up very strict rules about how to fill the time, realizing at the age of eight that boredom, not illness, could be the death of me. My aunt Maime or was it my aunt Katy, was cleaning out an attic one day and came across a set of *The Book of Knowledge*, printed around

1917. They arrived at my house, and what a day it was! In those twelve volumes was all that a civilized child was thought to need to know. How locomotives worked and the Laplanders lived and how to read French and make candle lanterns and who Tolstoy was and what his house looked like. They afforded me an insight into worlds that by the time I read about them two world wars and the ubiquitousness of television had altered irrevocably, but what a glorious world. And so winter became permanently fixed in my mind as a time for creativity and imagination. In January, the spirit of creativity has won and I wanted to be out in it, like the children sledding down the hill beneath my bedroom window I used to watch with envy and longing; and indoors reading a history of mathematics or an English mystery from the thirties, eating fudge in front of the fire, or upstairs in my yellow studio, designing quilted drapes for my bedroom. So many wonderful things to think about, so many wonderful things to make and do.

I found a set of that *Book of Knowledge*, a little more updated, at Ken Kelso's. The French lessons were the same, as were the literature, poetry, and drawings, but the skirts no longer swept the floor in the illustrations for science projects, and the Laplanders were gone. I bought the set for five dollars and from time to time take a volume down. Are children today expected to know as much of the world and the things that are in it as those children of 1917 or even 1932?

By spring that feeling of limitless creativity and intellectual boundlessness has left me. The gardens and the yards and the fencing and the demands of the season that draw me outside are so engaging and involving that I forget, and in doing so, in part forget who I am. The sheep have taught me hard lessons about truth. What is the truth of something? Am I loath to go to the barn in the cold winter's night to tend to them or simply loath to carry sloppy buckets of water down the stairs into the barn? I am loath to carry the water, of course; therefore, the sheep are safe and shall stay, and all I need to do is solve the water problem. Is it the winter I dread, or the problems that come with it? Solve the problems or at least manage them better and then look at the winter in a fairer light.

This morning the sky is crystal clear and blue. The snow gleams. The sun is that much higher in the sky than it was yesterday. The day that much brighter. All things carry within them the seeds of hope and the despair of winter in varying degrees, according to our circumstances. But in my heart today is hope.

TOMATO SOUP

AN INCREDIBLE soup was made today. In France, when you see the words *bonne femme*, a phrase that defies translation in American and English cookbooks but is often written as "good wife," it means that potatoes will be prominent in the dish. And so this soup has earned the designation of *bonne femme* affixed to *tomate*.

It began with the blue enamel wood stove which has an opening on its top to accommodate the large Swedish copper pot used for soups. Into it went butter, a lump the size of a pigeon's egg, and three or four onions, cut quite finely. They spent some time simmering on the stove until barely melted and then were joined by coarsely cut up chunks and diced peeled red-skinned potatoes, two store-bought chicken bouillon cubes, about four cloves of garlic, two bay leaves, some basil, and the entire contents of a one quart bag of tomato sauce made and frozen last fall for just such a day as this.

It simmered on the stove, filling the kitchen with its memories of both summer's joys and winter's comforts. Every time I came in from the barn, the smell rising from that pot was deeper and richer. Lunch. Maybe.

Life on the farm has been heading on a reckless, out-of-control course that happens only in the winter but not until February has come. Large crises blurred the edges of small details, and the barn is beginning to show the signs. Little things like a glove dropped in the press of ewes who were being given water just a little bit later than usual and whose anxious shuffling almost knocked me down, a bottle of corn syrup placed precariously in the dark while climbing down the ladder being knocked over and broken. A young ewe lying in a favored corner with her lambs nursing, observed but not noted. An old ewe dropping a lamb in the windiest spot in the barn after breaking through a gate in an attempt to obtain privacy. The lamb being rushed to the house and soaked in the warm-water-filled sink, tube-fed egg yolk mixed with corn syrup and milk replacer, wrapped in a sweatshirt with a plastic tonic water bottle used as a hot-water bottle and having its temperature taken every ten minutes until it rose from 93 degrees to the normal 103 degrees. The ewe, in the meantime, dropped a second lamb in the very dry, very protected, crowded, comfortable corner of the barn from which she so recently escaped in order to drop the first lamb.

Shall we add sixty-some-odd bales of hay being left on the doorstep, the snow having blocked the route to the barn, blocking all exits from the house, necessitating climbing over them while carrying two bottle lambs and their formula, bales being hauled almost three hundred feet to the barn with me acting as cart horse, pulling them balanced on a toboggan and all the while the smell of that soup, enjoyed but not partaken of, permeating the kitchen as I prepared a bottle to tempt the lambs of the ewe who had not moved from her favorite spot in the corner?

The hay is now moved and stacked. The animals are fed. The kitchen pipes, frozen for a day, are once more thawed. The new puppies fed three times. The water for the barn is drawn. The sheep can no longer make it to the brook, nor the culvert, for that matter, and eagerly wait the 150-odd gallons of water to be poured out for them. And, of course, all fires are kept going, and the wood for them brought in to fill their respective wood boxes. And the smell of that soup wafts through the house.

Suddenly I remember that there are two lambs too many in the main part of the barn, and that if the ewe lying down (whose name is Daisy, by the way) really hasn't gotten up, she must be terribly thirsty. So back down to the barn to give her water and find the mother of the two extra lambs.

Daisy can't stand up. I half lift, half drag her away from the bedding she's fouled and put clean straw under her and give her water, a quart at a time, between feeding the others more hay. The water is given in intervals, in order not to shock the thirsty ewe's system. Her ewe lamb, no matter how gently persuaded, won't take more than an ounce from the bottle. I put everyone into the cozy dry part of the barn and suddenly hear the ewe struggling. She's dying. Oh, no! I run to her and see her flailing her legs convulsively. I pull the ewe to her feet. She stands. Slowly she begins to eat the hay that was set before her a few minutes earlier.

I tuck the lamb in a jacket, tie the sleeves, and carry her up the ladder, past the sixty newly stacked bales of hay, into the warm house with all fires glowing brightly. In the kitchen, where the soup is still warming, I take a silver demitasse spoon from a drawer and feed the lamb four ounces of milk, a spoonful at a time, go back outside, get some very sweet-smelling hay from the broken bale still lying on the front door stoop, and put the weak lamb, as well as the other two bottle-fed lambs, on to the hay. Then, noting that the clock is announcing the ninth hour after noon and the twenty-first hour of the day, take a ladle from the drawer and stir the soup on the stove, ladle some into a big blue-and-white cup, and sit down in front of the living room fire, legs over the arm of the overstuffed chair, and eat *potage tomato à la bonne femme*, tomato soup!

EPIPHANIES AND OTHER MOMENTS

S UNDAY MORNING was a special time for me. My reward, in a way, for the year and especially for yesterday, an intense, tension-ridden, and nearly too-difficult-for-words day of shearing. It shouldn't have been. I had hired a shearer who was a bit on the temperamental side. A prima donna, the Emperor of the sheep-shearing world. Or so he thought. All seventy-one sheep who were to be shorn and their lambs had been penned inside the day before, as he had requested. Shearing wet sheep is difficult. He had also requested that they not be fed or watered for twenty-four hours before he came. Since he would be shearing for at least eight hours, it was too much stress for my nursing and pregnant ewes, so I split the difference. And in they went for twelve hours. I made certain there was fresh bedding that they could nibble on. Hay, in other words. He would know they had eaten.

Moments before the Emperor of Shearing arrived, a van pulled into my driveway. In it was a family sent to me by the nearby Hanford Mills Museum. The museum had canceled its Sheep to Shawl Day and sent me a family that had wanted to see shearing. They were speaking with me when the Emperor of Sheep Shearers appeared in a huff. Late for him, but two hours early for our appointment. He had skipped his morning shearing. I was as ready for him as was possible, except I hadn't started the pear tart that was to be for the shearing dinner.

I now have a new green picket fence around my south pasture. It is complete and reaches all the way to the barn. There is a nice alleyway from my driveway right down to the apple green gate leading to the barnyard. Gates into the field are not yet hinged but are tied and look to be as complete as they should be. Without a pause the shearer drove up to the apple green gate leading into my field. His son got out of the truck, untied the gate, and the Emperor drove through and into my pasture. "Why are you driving there?" I asked.

"To get to your barn," he responded.

"You can't get there from here," I replied in true Yankee fashion. "Why not?" Well, that set the tone for the day, or at least the morning through lunch.

It went from bad to worse. Suddenly the setup that the Emperor last year had found adequate was now a subject of ridicule and rage. The sheep began to panic. I wasn't certain that they would get shorn. The neighbor's children who came to watch and help, the family from the museum, my neighbor Herb Klumpe who brought his friend's sheep to be shorn all stood on eggs, whole, unboiled, fragile-shelled eggs, in an effort not to make a sound, the sound of not even one egg cracking to upset this sputtering shearer. Instead, they lifted eyebrows, gestured to me, and tiptoed out of the barn.

I had prepared most of the dinner for the Emperor and his heir-designate at five o'clock that morning. "Go make lunch," he decreed. "By the way, I'm only trying to teach you how to do things right," he added.

And so the Emperor and his heir-designate came up to the house, washed, and sat down. I served a homemade fromage au poivre (cracked pepper and chive cheese), fresh milk from my cow, home-made bread an hour out of the oven, a veal dish with tomatoes and olives, a salad, and a pear tart with fresh cream from my cow, coffee, and a pitcher of ice-cold milk. We went back to the barn. There was nary a grumble after that.

Shearing is one of the definitive moments in a shepherd's year. It is a time for assessment and evaluation. Once the fleeces are off you can see how your flock fared the winter: who needs something extra, who is bred, who is okay. I got several surprises. About eight ewes are very pregnant. As of today I have fourteen May lambs. That is seven more than last year, with eight ewes still pregnant. The flock, with the exception of five ewes in trouble, are from good to excellent on a condition score, as decreed by the shearer himself, or rather the Emperor, much better than last year. Last year was one of our worst winters, nonetheless, this year's group was on a three-lambings-in-two-years self-starter program. We got full fleeces from all seventy-one that he sheared. Last year five of the fleeces were in pieces.

The major health indicator of sheep is the condition of their fleeces. When a sheep has poor nutrition or suffers stress, the fleece will be weak and break at the spot where it was growing when the poor nutrition or stress occurred. If the nutrition and stress are really severe, a yellow line will develop and run through the fleece. There were only two sheep out of seventy-one with any break in their fleece. Both surprises, yearlings who otherwise looked good. The third indicator from a sheep's fleece about a flock's health is volume of fleece. This winter was not a particularly cold one, yet the Emperor decreed that I had at least fifty percent more fleece from the flock than I had at last year.

The fleeces were weighed, evaluated, and graded at the Wool Pool today. The Emperor was right. My fleeces graded top grade, except for some belly wool, and weighed fifty percent more than last year. Considering that I kept back five to use for hand spinning, that is quite good.

Well, it would seem the Emperor really needed his dinner, because the afternoon's shearing simply became a monologue about sheep from the expert's mouth. I listened and smiled, and listened, and continued to pen sheep for him until he was finished. "I sheared 750 sheep in three days before coming here," he said. It would seem to be by way of apology. "See you next year," said the Emperor of Shearing. I laughed. My daughter said I should have served dinner at eleven in the morning rather than one-thirty in the afternoon. However, this lady of the manor never invited the Emperor of Shearers to set foot on this farm again.

SAMANTHA

A CAR SCREECHED to a sudden stop on Elk Creek Road a couple of days ago, late afternoon. The familiar sound of a country tragedy. It is the sound of fear. The sound of terror, in fact. My son rushed out of the house. He saw a car stopped in the middle of the road. A man got out. My younger dog, Samantha, came racing toward the house from the roadside, ran to Joachim for a brief moment to be petted, only then to desperately circle the house and disappear into my farm office. The man drove off without a word.

I had left for work leaving Joachim with the two dogs. Joachim called me later in the evening at my job. "I can't find Samantha," he said, "anywhere." He had searched the house, most of its cellars, the farm office, the wood room, and finally, with a neighbor's flashlight, along the roadside ditches, he said, after retelling the story of the accident. The accident that we were not certain had happened. Was Samantha hit, grazed, or missed? Border Collies are the smartest dogs of all, I've been told, and yet they are quite often roadside casualties in the country. The instinct to herd, to work, is built in, bred, some say for hundreds of years, and others, thousands. There is a school of thought that the Norwegians brought elk-hunting dogs with them to England and crossed them with some herding dogs from France, and there is another school of thought that links them with the wolf. Above all, Border Collies need to work. It is ingrained in them to flock something, anything. Even cars moving quickly along the road.

Samantha had been taught, with her mother Steele, to drop on the verge of the road upon hearing an approaching vehicle. I realized early on that since Border Collies are driven to *do something* when a moving object approaches or recedes from them, to train them to drop on the wayside grass was a possible replacement action to chasing cars. Steele can be trusted, but Samantha is still very young, and I'm not certain what she will do if I'm not with her. The shepherd acts as a command dog.

Samantha is an eager and loving puppy. The first sound of my step in the driveway coming home will bring her running to me. If I so much as mention her name to someone with whom I'm talking on the phone, Samantha will react to me from the back porch. She reads my mind and comes to me when I've just thought her name, before I can even call "Sammie, Sam, Sam." She is always there. Until the other evening.

My boss was most understanding about the phone calls interrupting us all evening. "Did you look here, did you look there, the other where . . ." I asked, bringing up every imaginable other either Joachim or I could think of, but no Samantha.

The next morning I came home directly from work and walked beside all of the roadside drainage ditches. I looked in the big metal culvert under the road, and then, with an enticing piece of cooked chicken held in my hand, went into the wood room where sometimes Samantha sleeps far underneath a set of stairs. The room was silent except for the beat of my heart. "Samantha," I called. I looked partway under the stairs. No Samantha. I turned to go back to the house proper to get a flashlight when, just then, I saw a tiny tip of a black nose emerge very slowly. She had been under those stairs all night and into the next morning. "Samantha." Her face appeared. She made no sound. I reached in and pulled her out. Half dragging, half carrying, I brought her into the morning light, a silent pup, with no apparent injuries, frightened silent, but fine. She came with me into the house, but it took some coaxing to get her to go up the stairs and into Joachim's room. "Jocko, wake up! It's Samantha!" And in a minute his face was covered with doggy kisses. Her tail energetically wagging, Samantha was very much alive. And still Sammie, Sam, Sam.

This afternoon, while shoveling out the barns, my son and I noticed a sheep way up on the hill, near the tree line. She was too still, sitting without moving for far too long. A short distance away was something white, not moving and less distinct. Joachim, ever practical, suggested I check with binoculars before walking up there. I never focus them correctly. He did. One sheep became distinct. The something white was obscured by a bush and less identifiable.

We took Steele and Samantha and went up to investigate. The side hill has been providing pasture for some time now and it was good to be able to inspect it at close range. As we went up to the tree line, we spotted a young ewe and an old ram that had separated from the flock and spent the day together. The something white was the ram that immediately joined the ewe to protect her.

They had chosen well. The view was beautiful. The hills are alive with color right now, and looking down, the proportions of the layout of my farm are pleasingly well ordered. Joachim and I searched for trees to become candidates for future Christmases. The dogs returned the ram and the ewe to the fold. The fear that the ewe was dying and the white spot was a lamb was a reasonable but erroneous one. They were safe. We all went down the hill for tea.

Fear doesn't leave me, when confronted by relief, as immediately as it once did. It lingers first in the center of my heart, and then, imperceptibly, moves out to its edges. Slowly I find myself hugging Samantha, unexpected bursts of love without apparent reason. And watch the flock with a sense of wary caution. Life and death are so immediate here on this farm, partly because there are so many of us, sheep and lambs and dogs and cows and me, and all so much out of my control, in hands more wise than mine.

Tea was a rough kind of one for today. There was no time to bake. We had leftover cake and toasted cheese sandwiches. It was all in all a rough kind of day, mucking out the barn in a faint drizzle of rain. Climbing the side hill with rapid caution. But I was grateful for it. It was a good day.

ON RABBITS AND DEATH

THE RABBIT, the one by the last name of Pierce, whose first name is not as yet determined, the rabbit-colored one, gray, tan, beige, cream, brown all mixed together, the biggest one, the one who looks like every Beatrix Potter bunny that ever was drawn, has decided it likes me. The "it" is the key. I still don't know if it is male or female. That is why there is no first name to this young Pierce.

Nonetheless, it has decided it likes me. I can't imagine why. I don't understand rabbits any more than I understood sheep in the beginning. This rabbit had fallen out of the cage one day. I was horrified. I had gone to the rabbit cage and realized that two were missing: a white one and a rabbit-colored one. Under the cage cowered the white one. I reached out quickly, grabbed it, and put it back in the cage. That was easy, but the other rabbit blended in with the hay and wood and miscellaneous carriage house conglomeration. I couldn't find it, and every move I made created a tiny sound, although not too tiny for those long rabbit ears. It stayed silent, terrified, immobile, hidden. I gave up, and that broke my heart. I closed the doors to the carriage house as tightly as I could so the dogs wouldn't go in and terrify the rabbit and then left.

The next morning I went in, despair in my heart, dreading what I might find, to feed the other rabbits. There in a corner was the rabbit-colored one. It took one look at me and hid. I put out food and water for it, unable to figure out how to catch it. I have a friend, Linda Jones, who manages to find a practical solution to most animal problems. Sometimes those solutions don't work, however, not because the solution itself is impractical but because of a peculiarity on my farm. She suggested putting food under a box that would be propped up with a stick. "The stick should be tied to string. When the rabbit goes under the box, pull the string, the stick drops, the box encloses the rabbit, and there you have it." Not to say that I had a box.

I went back every day for a few days. The rabbit stared at me. I stared at it. It came close, but if I moved, it moved away. One day, being behind schedule, I forgot to leave the rabbit any food. There was plenty in the cage for the others but none for this little one. I was less afraid that it would starve than apprehensive about its discovering the delights of eating out. Outside, that is, of the carriage house; in other words, escape into the wild. I ran into the carriage house, a plate of lettuce, alfalfa pellets, and a dish of water in hand. I placed them on the floor and sat down near them, my hands outstretched. The rabbit scurried around where I sat. It then looked at me, motionless. I was as still as I could be. The rabbit approached. Oh, I had put the food too far away for me to grab the rabbit. The rabbit slowly moved closer. Neither of us took our eyes off one another. It slipped up to my hand. It stood absolutely still, its long angora fur touching my hand. I moved with great caution, and I put it back in the cage.

In the time between starting to write about the rabbit and finishing writing about the rabbit, I got a phone call. Calls about death in my family come between seven and seven-thirty in the morning, so one can have one last night's sleep before facing the truth.

I hadn't known my aunt was as sick as she was. My family is a Yankee one. We, or rather, they, don't say too much about that kind of thing, terminal illnesses, death, even divorce. Divorce is still a whispered word in my family. Ofttimes it seems I say too much about everything, but there are some things essential to me that can't be pried out of me on pain of death. I am my mother's daughter.

My aunt was a very old lady. I would have liked so much to have been told that she was sick. I couldn't have made her well, but I could have driven her crazy just one more time, by sending her flowers or something to brighten her day. "You shouldn't have. You can't afford it. I don't need them," would have been the response. "You're making a demand on me to reply to you," would have been the implication. But her heart would have been touched and I would have preferred to know I sent my living aunt flowers rather than a bouquet to a funeral home.

When my mother died, I bought flowers. Lots of them. And made little bouquets and tied them with ribbons. I went to the cemetery where most of my family is buried, outside of New London, and put those bouquets on everyone's graves: my grandparents and uncle and great-uncle and sister and father and mother.

I live on a farm, and life and death are a daily part of my existence. As timely a thing as the clover seeds I planted, frost sowing. Did they live or did they die? Lambs, sheep, rabbits, goats, pigs, dogs, a cat, and a cow. Grass, seeds, trees, flowers. Did they make the winter? Did they live or die? I am fortunate in being able to see all rhythms of life each day. A life on a farm does not remove one from what is basic to human life. Which is the moment, or rather, when is the moment in life when one becomes resigned? When one gives up? When one knows that all of the effort in the world won't make things any better? It happens in some of us at the end. In some, way before the end. In some, at the beginning. In a few, it never happens. To die becomes a more rather than a less. To face God, a joy, a beginning rather than an end.

My mother was one of seven children. We were never told if

there were any others. It would be strange in those days of childhood disease unbuffered by vaccinations if there were not one or two who didn't make it. Those seven were intensely close with each other and distant from everyone else. They protected us children, we were told, but in fact themselves from information about one another that wasn't exactly suitable for us to know. So, in many ways, we didn't know them. And if we did discover one of their secrets and told them we did, they said it was a product of a vivid imagination. Even were it something they had, in some amazing lapse, told us.

Spoken words had power. Written ones even more. "Never put it in writing," my mother cautioned. "I burn all of your letters on the stove," she'd say. Her gas cooking stove. "All of my letters about the farm!" I'd wail. "In case there was something in them," she'd whisper.

And so I wasn't told my aunt was dying. As if saying so would make it true.

It rained here today. The last of April. I have to go to the barn now, to set it up for a relief milker for my one cow and to make things easier in order for someone else to do my chores. I am to be away for the funeral tomorrow.

Rabbits, pigs, goats, sheep, dogs, cat, and cow. The daffodils from my garden won't travel well from here to Connecticut. I wish I could bring them, tied in little bows, to the cemetery.

TO MILK THE COW

TO MILK the cow, properly, that is, one first must make cheese or yogurt from yesterday's milk, so the spare pail into which one periodically dumps the milk from the stainless steel bucket while milking, should the cow become restless and consider kicking said bucket, will be available. To weed the flowerbed efficiently, without planting anything new, one must clean the carriage house. To arrive at that requirement takes a more circuitous route. You see, next to the carriage house is a pile of boards. The boards were left from last year's slab woodpile. They are quite usable. They are piled fairly close to the carriage house itself. They are there because it is too difficult to mow the lawn up to the building's edge. Therefore it was less than a good idea but nonetheless an expedient place to store them. Temporarily. Another way to avoid mowing up to the drip line of the building, and not have to weed to the edge, is to plant a double row of sweet cicely. Sweet cicely grows thick and bushy, flowers once, gets cut back, and grows large fernlike leaves for fall. I have a lot of it in the flower garden. Too much all needing badly a new place to live.

There also are many small plants in the garden path. I used to weed the garden and try to save thinnings to plant somewhere else, but they'd die before I'd get the place they were to be moved to prepared. Therefore, I cleaned part of the inside of the carriage house where the boards are to go, moved the boards inside, had my helper dig holes where the cicely is to go, and mixed in manure. So when the snow melts off, I can weed the garden and transplant all of the seedlings and larger plants to the now-ready-to-plant side of the carriage house.

To clean the kitchen to be ready for the summer is still another task. To do that, I must first clean and whitewash the root cellar as well as unboard the windows. We've had a lot of rain and the third room of the cellar is damp. So I must unboard the windows to help dry out the root cellar and throw out all of the outdated paint and things on the shelves next to it, and rake the rubble from the floor where an oil tank once stood (although that might be going too far) and whitewash the inside of the root cellar. *That* isn't going too far, because those shelves are needed on which to store the many bottles and jars that I save for jams and vinegars. It will be time-consuming to move them when I do need to whitewash the shelves.

Which brings me to the kitchen. It is an old-fashioned one. Big. Airy. With very little storage. I have one old pine cupboard that is original to the house that holds everything that isn't food. Gradually it has assumed its own set of uses, and functions (if I can glorify anything in my house as something that functions) to serve the most immediate needs of the kitchen. An entire shelf is filled with cookbooks. Another houses linens and plates piled in order of size. Two others, however, hold miscellany. Some French clay baking dishes that are too valuable to put in the larder and risk breaking. Cups, glasses, a special set of cookie cutters, my grandson's, to cut out a train. And on top, a pile of broken dishes that are too valuable to throw away and that I never seem to find time to mend.

Then there are the two bottom shelves. They are the kind of shelves that when you open the door, everything falls out. What that everything is is hard to tell. It is the kind of everything that you think you need and must have and yet never use, because you forget you have it, because you never see it, because it is on one of the shelves where everything falls out when you open the door.

I empty those shelves "once and for all" on occasion, usually once a year. Sometimes twice. And rant and rave when I need something and find myself emptying it all out onto the floor. And rant and rave even more when I throw it all back in, saying, "Tomorrow I'll do it right." Well, those things can go on the shelves next to the root cellar, or on the root cellar shelves, after they're whitewashed, of course.

Which brings me to the barn. Because the carriage house has been neatened in order that the garden can be weeded, I can tidy the tools that have somehow found their way to the barn and hang them neatly in the carriage house. The Yankee in me thinks all of their handles should have been rubbed with linseed oil this winter when I sat by the fire in the evening, but, of course, that didn't happen. One of the boys who works for me might do them and they can be returned to their proper place.

But more important to the farm is a retaining wall that cannot be improved until some manure is first moved to make the pumpkin hills. That is a wall that the sheep can hop over to come onto my lawn, gardens, and eventually the neighbor's lawns and gardens from the pastures. It forms the short end of the barn bridge. They notice it every year. They haven't this year as yet; however, they soon shall. A deep trench was dug out in front of it in an effort to locate the water line to the barn. There had been cicely plants there before it was dug and it looked very pretty. The dirt remained in a pile in front of the trench. It was especially good dirt because it was once my compost pile. I want the trench dug deeper in order to expose more of the wall, and then hope to build the wall higher so that the sheep won't go over it. Therefore, in order to build up the wall I have to have the west aisle of the barn shoveled out. And as the aisle is shoveled, it has to be dumped in rows in my field. The dirt from beside the stone wall is to be put on top of the manure piles. I shall then plant Rouge Vif d'Etampes pumpkins on the piles and some decorative corn and some sugar corn, and some scarlet runner beans to climb to the top of the corn.

It snows. And it's sticking, this twelfth day of May. Seven months this year saw snow on the ground. I've kept some bagging ewes indoors, penned, because I don't want them to freshen outside. The temptation is there to let them out, because the barn is so very overcrowded. The sheep, in their short coats, don't want to go outside. So they crowd in the warmest part of the barn. Sheep like to lamb in a private place; therefore, the outdoors may easily become a private place to them. This is a moment of transition for us here on the farm. The calendar and some manifestations of nature, albeit not the temperature, attest to that.

I have examined the problem of choosing between expediency and order over a long period of time. Sometimes what is expedient both at Greenleaf and on the farm makes sense and in some instances works out, but this year the sheep and I are going to try an experiment. I am committing myself to order and logic and am not going to be tempted by expediency, however appealing. That means I turned down a convincing and well-meaning offer to help with the bridgeway wall combined with the refusal to shovel the aisle. We'll take our chances. At least I'll have what is done, done right. Halfway measures will be avoided. All farmers are looking at tough times ahead. The weather has been against us for almost a year. I've carefully considered the future of this farm, and my decision has been made. I shall shovel the aisle before building the stone wall. And in all ways I shall choose order over expediency whenever possible. It shall make the difference.

WATCH AND YOU WILL KNOW

E LLIOT THE duck arrived last night. She is a delight. And quite a famous duck, a duck extraordinare. I'd never noticed ducks before. Oh, yes, I saw one in *Babe*, but that was definitely of the Daffy variety. Not one that a person could be particularly fond of, no matter how eloquently he stated his case. So it was with some surprise that I greeted Elliot in my wood room last night. A note on my kitchen table told me she was there, but I wasn't expecting the delightful creature that greeted me at the door. Her beak is gray, her feathers light buff and not a bit of orange anywhere. Not one's typical bird. And chatter, oh, did she chatter. The variety of sounds that came from that little feathered creature as she rushed to greet me was enchanting. Until that moment, I had absolutely no idea about the conversational abilities of ducks. The proprietorship of Elliot includes the acquiring of her friend, Kitty Hawk, who is not ready to be brought to Greenleaf yet. She shall arrive soon. The two have been friends since they were babies. Kitty Hawk is a cat. If she is remotely as charming as her friend Elliot, I'm going to have a wonderful time with them both. And some duck eggs, too.

Three new sheep have arrived. A yearling and a pair of two-year-old twin sisters. Romney-Finn crosses with some Dorset blood. One has the thick, long, dark Romney fleece. When they came, they panicked a little upon leaving the truck, and one literally took to the hills. She raced up the hills of my neighbor across the road, up and down, and around my neighbor's house and pigpen, to the fascination of my neighbor's dog. A grand adventure was had by all. Some skillful handling brought the sheep back across the road, down the slope, through a gate I haven't used in a year. Off she went to join her new flock. The new sheep haven't been named. They shall be. Their names simply haven't occurred to me yet.

From the start they have stayed together, a tiny flock, giving comfort to each other, with memories of their prior home. This morning they were in Sheep Meadow with the other sheep, goats, cows, and pigs. I crossed the beautiful new bridge under its canopy of apple branches and walked through the flock on my way up the hill. "Cahm ahn," I said, "Cahm ahn." The new black sheep started toward me. "Cahm ahn." And led the flock single file up the hill to the summer pasture. The morning grass was thick and lush with dew. The shadow of the mountain darkened the meadow. Tall trees at the edge of the stone walls sheltered us. There is ample grazing for them up here.

The goats separated from the sheep and followed me when I slipped into the woods. The sheep stayed in the meadow, intent upon the thick rich grass. I wanted to see the huge old apple trees by the stone wall surrounding my little woods. To see where they have been going, of late, in the afternoons. The trees were thick and dark, arching over the walks and quiet places they have made. The goats followed me down the hill.

Bringing the sheep to pasture has been part of a shepherd's life for thousands of years. I have been getting better at it as time goes on. This year I've been singing to them. They don't seem to mind my voice. And this year it has been a gentler experience. They have begun to follow me, nearly single file, at a steady pace, rather than the gallop they sometimes used to do. Sitting with them in the pasture gives me a chance to see how they are. Who is fat enough, who is thin, who is bagging. Three look as if they shall be coming in soon. I've drawn bright shocking pink stripes down their backs so they can be spotted more easily. Some of the older ewes look big, too. But they are not bagging.

My friends in Hamden have taken some of my sheep for the summer. They love sheep. It is a relief to my pasture as well. Theirs have had a good boost from fertilizer and lime and look really good. The sheep were terrified in the barn as they were caught and brought on the truck. The second of the two truckers, a man and his fourteen-year-old son, were particularly gentle with them, but fear had already set in. Some of my favorites are over for my friends to enjoy. Patricia Fitz Roberts and her brother Prinz Rickart, Hope McKenzie, and my Cornell Finns. Six ewes and one fine Finn ram belonging to my friends went, too. They live here part of the time. Two lambs I bought from another friend are also there. To be tamed and treated as special. Thank you, Liz and Arthur.

The brush that has jumped the stone wall around the woodlot is going to provide a new fence to surround the barnyard. I saw a picture in a decorating magazine of a farm fence in Austria-Hungary. It was made from saplings woven, still green, through those horizontal bars. I want that fence. As the green wood dries it becomes a force to tighten the pressure on the horizontals against the post. My newfound carpenter and his son will go up to the woodlot on their four-wheelers, cut down saplings, except for the oak, and build it for me. For us.

The chickens arrive in a day or two. I hope to be ready for them. Twelve chickens and three chicks. And the famous Tucker. Tucker is the world's most glorious rooster. His feathers gleam and shine all of the iridescence that a rooster can sport. I wanted him from the very moment I ever saw him. He belonged to a good friend. And it was wrong for me to want him so badly. But I mixed the feelings with admiration and a sure knowledge that I'd someday have one of his boys. It is dawn. Tucker must be awakening now on his home farm. But in another day he shall find himself on mine.

This is that watchful time. For what happens in the summer affects the winter and the life that is lived then. I watch for signs of parasites and foot problems. For the overall condition and for the healthy shine on the sheep's faces. I watch to see who is tame and who needs some extra attention. And watch in that silent watch that I've learned is the essence of being a shepherd. A watching that uses no words to accompany or describe it but places the images of what is seen like flat sheets of tissue paper in a drawer ready to wrap gifts to be opened in the days and nights still left to be on this farm.

ROSE

THE OLD ewe rose to her feet and stamped the front right one at me. Stamp. Stamp. She sighted the dogs with her good eye, or did she hear them first? A low rumbling sound came from deep in her throat. She faced off the dogs knowing I was the lesser of the two threats. After all, although I had brought her pain, I had also hand-fed her, and perhaps had brought some relief as well. The dogs, on the other hand, commanded her to move where she didn't want to go.

I had gone up the side hill to the edge of Sheep Meadow to search for her dead body. It was time, I thought. It had to be all over. The vet had come and couldn't help. I had called him twice. "This is not nursing care any longer," I had said. "This is a job for a vet." She had lost a horn. I don't know how. This Horned Dorset who was to become the mother of my future Horned Dorset flock. And the flies, so prevalent in August, had laid their eggs in the convenient hole left by the horn. I had penned her, treated her with Pine-Sol and peroxide. I dared not put tar on it for fear of driving the larvae that much farther in. A screwworm bomb is often successful, but I couldn't find one locally. Anywhere. For more then a week, there was a message left on my answering machine to greet everyone who called ". . . please get me a screwworm bomb." The ewe stayed in the barn for a while and then began to hide outside. I treated her daily, while inside, with peroxide. The Pine-Sol seemed to irritate more than it helped. A week ago I found her. The skin had been rubbed raw on that side of her head. The fleece was worn off her neck. She was in agony. She had begun to eat grain from my hand when in the barn. She also associated me with the dreaded wound and my unsuccessful efforts to help. It was then that I made my second call to the vet and begged him to come.

The next morning she was with the flock by the side of the barn. Her left eye was closed. Her neck was bleeding. I got a loop over her head and the remaining horn. She couldn't see me when I approached. She fought a little harder than I did. She is a little stronger and a bit heavier than I am. She is certainly a wily old ewe. Low-slung. Strong. All I wanted from a Horned Dorset. A fighter. Tough. The most powerful animal I've had in the barn. But I had one thing over her. While she was trying to save herself from the short-term agony she suspected she'd have to endure, I was trying to save her life. So despite the fact that she had it way over me in strength, I had it over her in power. I won.

I tied her to an apple tree and there she stayed until the vet's truck pulled in. The maggots didn't leave when he squirted a medicine in and didn't leave when he put an antiseptic on the wound. She kicked and fussed and he couldn't get close. "She wasn't raised here," I apologized. "If there were only something to keep the flies off," he said. "Can we use Ectiban?" I asked. "It works on the cow to keep the flies off her." I hadn't used it before because I didn't think it could be used on a raw wound. It shouldn't be in the bloodstream. The vet said to get it. I did. The ewe stood still for me while I scratched it into her fleece and dusted her head. I talked slowly to her. She listened to me. It will never cease to amaze me. Ever. I really can never understand why it happens. Or how.

I slipped her out of her noose and off she went. Up across the brook. Up the meadow to the shelter of the cool dark stone wall. I saw her grazing there a couple of times. But she'd disappear before

I'd get close enough to check the wound. The day before yesterday, I didn't see her at all.

For the past three weeks, since she lost the horn, I'd felt a lingering sense of being out of control. A sense of failure. It crept into my heart when I least expected it and without warning. I didn't connect it with the ewe, just with circumstances beyond my control that were a bit too much for me this past month. Late yesterday afternoon, my grandson and I went elderberry picking along the stone walls. I'd been telling him about my grandfather Wolf's elderberry wine. And how I must gather enough berries to make some. A woman stopped me on the road to ask directions. She'd never been here on Elk Creek before. "How pretty," she said, delighting in its loneliness. I knew any delight I had had left me. For a while, at least.

Time to find the ewe. Time to bury her. I'll be brokenhearted until I do it. I got a small bag of grain. Just in case. Steele, Samantha, and I walked up the hill. She was nowhere to be seen. Suddenly, from behind the rock pile surrounded by a ring of seven young trees, there she was. Stamp. Stamp. Stamp went the right foot. Stamp. Stamp. Stamp.

The sixth anniversary of my mother's death is next week. Each year my heart fails me around now. Life does not seem possible. All sadness becomes too much to bear. The suffering ewe had become entangled in my heart with the sorrow I felt at the loss of my mother. But the ewe was alive. More than alive. The ragged bleeding skin was gone. And in its stead was clean pink new skin. A bit swollen, but flesh, clean, healthy. Her eye was open. There was not a fly to be seen. She stamped her foot at me and roared a deep guttural roar at the dog. I hadn't known how much despair had filled my heart until it lifted. And I was free once more.

This morning I took another bag of grain up the hill. She hadn't come close enough to me to eat yesterday's. I also took a small thermos of coffee in case I had a wait. She and I had to connect today.

She was asleep under a tree I particularly love. It has a fallen branch across a stone wall. It is a perfect place to sit. The branch is just the right height for me. I was prepared to spend the morning if need be. She let me approach. I fed her grain in my hands. She has a funny Dorset face. Sturdy. Chunky. Homely. One eye is glazed. The other is alert. She ate all the grain from my hands. I climbed into the crook of the tree and had my coffee. I decided to name her Rose, after my mother. For the moment, all is well again.

RUGOSA ROSES

R UGOSA ROSES, magenta to cerise, are still in bloom on the beach in Connecticut. Not many, but a few, here and there among the leaves. The rose hips are almost ripe. Some have become the dark orange that sets so well against the green leaves. The rest are still wearing a touch of light green, graduating to yellow and orange. I picked a few, just enough to fill my pockets, and make a glass of jam for my daughter. Enough to make a memory or two. And I couldn't resist picking one perfect bloom to give my cousin Marilyn.

Into another pocket went a shell. I don't remember when I last walked on a beach. Silken sand. The ocean roaring into shore. A long time ago, I spent every summer day running on the sand, racing in between the waves. Children run into the water as waves pull away and run out again as waves return. Laughing. Tiny gestures of mastery and power. I'm faster than *that* wave. I'm faster than the ocean. We built sand castles and ate sandwiches and stayed out of the water, prisoners of our mothers' fears. We wore little leather slippers so our feet wouldn't get cut from the shells. I hated those little slippers. To this day I go barefoot beyond the limits of common sense.

The sound of waves coming in crashes into this still quiet room, where the only sound is that of the pen crossing the page. I used to hold my breath and count how long the space was between the waves. The beach had been a bit of ordinary heaven. A familiar pleasure, too familiar to be grand. But grand it seemed the other morning, picking rose hips and filling my pockets with them.

It wasn't my beach. It was my cousin's beach. Mine lay beyond the crescent of Crescent Beach, Niantic, at the place where the Thames River meets the Sound. On summer days, when we weren't at the farm, we'd climb into the big black Buick and drive to Ocean Beach. My parents chose a distant spot, "away" from everyone, on an inlet close to a tiny island, accessible in low tide. We were taught not to swim but walk, our heads held high like little turtles, bathing caps and sand shoes in place, laughing when a wave splashed over us but terrified in our hearts of being swept away.

When I got old enough to dare, I'd slip across the shallow inlet onto the tiny island, not more than a sand dune, I'm sure, and explore. The fear of the tide coming in between me and the safety of my parents spoiled it somehow for me, but I did it anyway. And never told my mother.

On the other days we'd go to the "fahm" and visit my grand-parents and cousins. My cousins were lucky to be allowed to stay overnight, while we lived too nearby ever to sleep over. Although now I don't exactly know why we never did.

Two of my cousins and the son of one of them went to visit my grandfather's farm with me on the day of the rugosa roses. We remembered, with varying degrees of detail, our lives there and the lives that had gone on before. We exclaimed about what was still there and what wasn't, how much smaller it seemed to Henry and Marilyn who had last been there longer ago than I. The pastures had been allowed to grow over. Not even a memory of a meadow for a cow, or the potato fields, or the old well remained. There were secret rocks that marked the place beyond which I would not venture into the woods. Those rocks linger in the pasture. And yet pasture does not even appear in dreams in those scruffy woods any longer.

I went behind the house and found an apple tree that had been there when I was a child. The apples fell one at a time at my feet. I put two of them in my pocket with hopes of eventually getting their seeds to grow. My nature never changes.

We saw the family graves, some of them. And graves of a world that has vanished for me forever. My cousins weren't raised in New London, but my brother and I were. And there before me were names, name after name, of people who had filled my childhood with a sense of security. To a child a day is forever, and the large solid people inhabiting those days were forever as well. The kind of life that was so rich and full of meaning then is over, a victim of itself, in fact. In a wish to create a "better" life, our parents, everyone's parents, traded in what was glorious about their past lives in exchange for the illusion of what was good in the present. And something became forever lost in the process. I came the closest of all of us to having that old life. I farm the land that none of the rest of us have chosen to have. My life is about sheep, not cows, although there are some cows in it, but it is a farm. I pick apples and elderberries and have a hint of a garden. I, of us all, live closest to the life on my grandfather's farm.

But there is a difference. Although I live not so very differently from the way my grandparents did then, my style is different, in form as well as content. But there is one more important thing that is different. There was family all around them. Friends. Relatives. Community. There were ties that could be broken only by death and even then continued. There were so many of us sitting around that table in those days. So many of us under those trees. I know, I know, the poverty and struggle were unfathomable, even for me, for whom my own farm is all too often on the thin edge of survival. And yet there was rich fullness of spirit in that place, that farm on Society Road near Perkins Corners in Niantic, Connecticut, that is wanting in the life we live today.

And so I am glad to have picked a rose for my cousin Marilyn. And I am glad that Henry tasted a rose hip even if he didn't like it. And that his son took home some gleaming stones from the beach, unpolished by the ocean. I'm glad my brother drove us all the way to Connecticut. And that my son was on time to meet us. I'm glad that my daughter and a friend were so willing to sit for three hours in a car too small to hold us all without the anticipation of being squashed. And that my former daughter-in-law let my grandson miss school to come and be with us. I'm glad my uncle Percy came to see us in the hotel. And that we met my cousins as they came off the ferry from Orient Point, waving and smiling. "Did you know in the corner of your heart," I asked my cousin Henry, "that we'd meet the ferry even though we didn't know which one you'd take?" "It wasn't in a corner," he replied. "I knew in my whole heart." And I'm glad for all of it. For all of it.

DOWN THERE

THE SUN comes quickly over the hills into the valley where I live. Sudden. Sharp. Clear. A brilliant golden burst of light explodes over the treetops and pours down the valley, turning snow and blades of grass alike into gold. Sunrise is brief here in these Catskills. No nuances here. No subtlety of shades of color or tones of shadow. Neither rose nor violet nor blue. Silver is reserved for crescent moons. And even that appears only in the evening. Winter.

The last stars disappear with a startling fervor. The day has arrived. But the tone of the light will blend with a seriousness, in between the moments of the day, and soon forgotten, as each moment passes, in its beauty.

The most beautiful place in the world to be at night is in the barn. Tonight, I wore a great deal of bulky paraphernalia and carried a thermos slung over my shoulders with a baling twine strap and a stainless steel milk pail near full of warm water for the new cow and a gallon of water in a plastic jug for a penned sheep, and a baby bottle for the warm milk in the thermos for a bottle lamb, and a plastic bag to carry grain back up to the lamb in the rabbit pen in the cellar. I was a bit proud of myself for carrying all of the above so easily.

The stainless steel milk pail slid away from me when I fell on the ice in front of the wooden stairs leading down from the back porch. I didn't get wet, except from the plastic magenta baby bottle when its nipple popped out in my pocket. I didn't drop the gallon jug, however. I just gave up on it. I left the stainless steel pail and then, cautiously, although I'd already proceeded as cautiously as I knew how, made my way past the wood pile, its tarp blowing madly in the wind, past the carriage house, its neighboring willow tree trying intently to fly into my face, and onto the sheet of ice preceding the first set of stone stairs leading to the barn.

I'd pruned the willow tree in the summer with foresight and care to create handholds across all such icy spots as well as the stone stairs leading to the middle level of the barn. But I had to get to those accessible branches first. Cautiously.

In winter, one's footprints slowly melt the snow and turn into slippery patches, reluctant to let go of their implications upon one's life. They melt evenly. And become particularly dangerous, with a vengeance, when covered with a thin layer of rapidly accumulating snow.

After making several trips a day to the barn to check on the sheep, and the lambs, and the cows (there are now two where there was always one plus or minus a calf), and the goat, and the ducks, and the geese, and the barn cats, and after making several trips each evening, and one, perhaps, in the night, throughout a winter, even a winter as mild as this one, many, many, many footprints have melted and melted again into one another. All contribute with distinction to the creation of the sheet of ice, leading to the stone stairs, leading to the barn.

The wind made itself felt by blowing snow up the stairs into my face. The cold was undistinguished. The torn corduroys I sometimes favor were covering unrespectably but adequately my long johns. I had layers of sweaters I had forgotten I owned beneath my jacket, and I wear a hat now. The cold was not to be noticed.

The wind replaced the attention the cold had custom to command. Fear had left me with the water as it spilled out of the milk pail. Curiosity took its place. Would I make it? Down there?

Through the dark of the haymow, I keep forgetting to replace the lightbulb, and to the ladder. The ladder is an essential part of the down of the down there. I used to be afraid of ladders, and steep stairs, and open drops.

There are two and a half other ways to go down there. One involves no stairs, except ones from my kitchen to the basement. It does, however, involve several doors inside the house, one farm gate copying an English one, first built in the sixteenth century, a long slope, and a door leading directly into the barn. The system is on the north side of the house. There is very little between my house and the North Pole on that side. One could say there is nothing between my house and the North Pole except the curvature of the earth. It is all covered with ice now. My water line runs there as well, of course.

The other way to go down there takes me down my steep porch steps, around the carriage house on the south side, down a gradual slope beneath massive pine trees, and down only one flight of icy stone stairs to the barnyard and the barn. The half bypasses the tiny garden gate and the icy stone stairs and uses, instead, a twelve-foot farm gate I had copied from a book written in 1884; it crosses the barnyard diagonally, only to lead me to the former milk house, now lambing room. It is the longest way into the barn when one is carrying things.

There is a third way, as well, to go down there. It entails going up. The main door to my barn is directly behind the back door to my house. In a straight line, it is about one hundred feet away. But it opens beyond the barn bridgeway, which is an uphill slope. The doors are massive. And heavy. They used to blow open with mighty crashes. And equally mighty regularity. They don't anymore. After seven years of "farming it," I found, in an old book, a way to build an ingenious lever system that traditionally held such doors in perfect accord. And shut.

I love going through those doors, and I love working the huge lever. But I use them as a last resort. Hay blocks the entrance to them at the moment. Even worse, some straw, now frozen under a hole in the roof, blocks the stairs down to the mow that leads to the ladder to the barn. I have to sit on the rounded pile of icy straw and slide toward the opening to the stairwell, hoping that one foot, at least, will hit the top stairs and that I will not fall down the whole flight.

This method doesn't work very well while carrying stainless steel milk pails filled with warm water for the new cow. When the barn bridgeway is covered with a sheet of ice, there is a twenty-foot drop on either side.

And so, tonight, I climbed down the ladder from the dark haymow. The snow blew in where the battens had fallen off. The wind howled, carrying the edge of fear in its wake into the soft lights of the barn's night. With faces looking up at me as I came down. The wooden shutters Art Hilton so skillfully made, kept all sounds of wind and fear from entering, and a great deal of the cold as well. I took off my hat and jacket and hung them on a tree twig coat hook. And walked throughout the barn, looking for signs of newly born lambs. A tiny little tin horn sound came from the north wall. The familiar announcement of a most recent arrival. I approached slowly. Any sudden movement could startle a sheep and that in itself could cause her to abandon her lamb.

There in a dark and cold corner were two lambs, huddled together in a small pile. Their dam had left them. The orange coating on the body of the bigger one told me she had had a very hard time delivering those two and wanted to have nothing more to do with them. Ever again.

Suddenly, there was another tin horn sound coming from beneath the hay chute. Cold air was whistling down on a very small lamb, it legs still partially encased in its placenta. I rubbed it down with a feed sack and some straw, trying to encourage it to stand. It wouldn't.

The twins continued to call out to the mother who had so abruptly abandoned them. Their voices were weaker. I put all three in the feed sack, slung it over my shoulder, and made my way up the ladder to the midlevel of the barn. Its door would lead me to the shortest way to the house. I got as far as a set of stone stairs. They were too icy to climb with the sack of lambs in my arms and no handhold. I circled behind the carriage house. It, too, was surrounded by ice. I once again slung the sack containing three very wet, very cold newborns over my shoulder, got down on my hands and knees, and, one hand holding the bailing twine tying it closed, crawled to the stairs of my front porch. They, too, are of stone, but there are only three of them. I got us all into the living room and shook the contents of the sack on to the floor in front of the fire. All three wet, cold lambs were still alive. We had made it.

DAYS OF GRACE

JUNE HAS arrived. It is both a gift and an obligation. While it is the sixth month, and the year cries out it is half over, in fact there are thirty more days to the halfway mark, a grace period, in more ways than one.

Spring did not really happen until yesterday, the last day of May. Warm breezes, sunny skies, mixed with haze. In a matter of the space between late morning and midafternoon, the lilacs in some friends' yards burst into bloom, filling the air with their astonishing sweetness. For a few moments this morning, I thought the year was half over, and it could have no hope of a redemption. All that had been left undone this year presented itself with a burden of guilt that was too much to bear. I like my house well scrubbed, spring cleaning done before the spring is even halfway through and the winter's debris and clutter gone from my mind and house. A tall order for one person. These past few months were more difficult than I had expected. While I thought I'd make a quick and easy adjustment after the five years I spent at a full-time job in addition to the farm, I didn't. And that in itself became disheartening.

The end of May is the first time in months that life seems possible again. That is, possible if I get up a little earlier, walk a little faster, write a little clearer, pick up scrap wood and kindling from the ground every time I pass some, take off my shoes every time I enter the house, put the laundry away immediately as it leaves the dryer, trim two, no three, no four, well, maybe six sheep's hooves a day, enjoy the day the Lord has made, and in all other ways, become perfect.

But there is indeed a grace period, before time becomes closer to winter once again. There are about thirty days to get ready to try and beat it. I have some theories about beating it that bear testing out. I have nothing to lose and everything to gain. One of the theories entails getting ready for it *now*. Today. Every day do something that will make next winter all that it could be. Put away small sums of money, for example, to not be in want. Gather pinecones for starting fires. Bring in the wood for my bedroom stove. Quilt some fabric for drapes. Plant lots of tomatoes for sauce to capture summer for my winter table. As easy as it sounds to me simply to make a list and cross items off, the days get swept away with all the requirements of running this kind of house and trying to bring prosperity to the farm. The task at hand is to remember that list and be certain to accomplish something on it each day.

Goslings are about to arrive on this farm. They've been ordered from Stamford Agway Farmer's Co-op. Pastured Geese are the last business here at Greenleaf. Now that the "Pastured Poultry" chickens are beginning to behave properly and lay eggs (they wouldn't until I changed their nesting material from second cutting to straw), I'm on to "Pastured Geese."

The chickens live in a pretty spectacular movable chicken coop out on the field and have actually put on a little weight as well as deciding to lay again. The theory is that in their movable house, they eat grubs, bugs, and grass in addition to grain, mash, and oyster shells, and fertilize the soil at the same time. While Pastured Poultry are reputed to eat less grain, mine are eating as much, if not more; they are healthier, lay better eggs, and reputedly taste as good as free-range chickens do in the fall, should you not want to winter them over. Some of mine have been in the portable coop for almost two weeks. They seem to have adjusted well.

I must say, while the eggs are as delicious as they were when the chickens were free-range, the chickens themselves look a lot better. Their view of the farm is different each day. Their diet varies according to every new positioning of the coop. The ground from which they are moved looks awful, but I've been assured that their droppings will do wonders to the acidy strawberry-covered patches that they have covered. Somehow, I believe it will work. Next shall come the goslings. As fond as I am of pâté, I love a Christmas goose even more. But this enterprise has a bit more going for it than that. Symbols have a way of enduring in one's life, sometimes hovering in the back of one's consciousness for a long time before seeing daylight and opportunity to become a reality rather than an idea. The second cookbook I owned as a young bride, recently married to an Air Force man and drafted into the role of cooking for him and his Air Force buddies, was Elizabeth David's *French Country Cooking*. It was an ideal book for a novice cook with three hungry young men at the table most evenings, because French food or, rather, French country food is highly flavored and very, very cheap to prepare. I won't mention how long it takes to create those recipes, however.

One of the dishes that became a standard in my repertoire was a Cassoulet de Castelnaudary. In it was something called confit, goose preserved in its own fat. Meats have been preserved that way for centuries. I couldn't find confit in any store, however, locating it attained monumental symbolic status in my mind. If I had a crockery jar of confit, I would be a real cook!

Hence, the imminent arrival of a respectable number of goslings. Oh, not all are for this winter's larder. Some shall go to New York to Dean and Deluca, a store that is interested in having both livers and confit. Some shall become gifts for the family. And one shall fill a stone crock in my larder next to the metal bread box and the bottles of elderflower vinegar.

One of the nicest things about having the chickens outside is that they bring me out into a field I don't frequent much. I pretend that I go to check on water or mash or grain. And they do have to be moved. But it really is to look at them. I get to see the brook and the apple trees in bloom and look at the new fence, still intent on being built, and in other ways be grateful for the day.

The goslings shall add still another dimension to the dream that is Greenleaf. Should the weather ever improve with any consistency, I shall have them out on the pasture as well, in a large movable coop. My daughter will research what to feed them to fatten their livers. And we shall have our own pâté as well as some to sell.

In today's mail shall go the first installment of cash for my dear brother to use when buying me some books for the next winter. The fabric for covers for the pillows in the library is being washed in the basement as I write. But there must be still another dimension to this day of grace. Winter skies will come soon enough. Each task done needs bring its own joy. And the day requires being lived well without fear of tomorrow. It is in gathering the beauty of each individual moment that one, in truth, gains strength for what the future holds. June. Days of grace.

THE STORY OF THE BARN

T HE SUNSET last evening held every variation of color and form that I have ever seen in a July sky. Feathers and stripes, combs and tails leading to nowhere conspired with the light to become all of the July evenings of my life, New England, New York City, and Central New York all in one dramatic display. Colors ranged with names such as hyacinth and cornflower and steel gray and purple, each touching the cloud formation in a way unique and glorious.

The sheep were well onto my neighbor Tom Connelly's second hill when I came down the back porch stairs into the evening. I sent Steele and Samantha out after them, all the while calling out to them. "Cahm ahn, cahm ahn." On command, the sheep turned on a dime and went rushing back home through the pink gate. Steele and Samantha didn't pick up fast enough and so were not behind them to drive them in. But I was glad of it. I wanted to watch them, graceful, single file. The flock slowed down before the bridge and proceeded to cross it with decorum born of necessity and good sense.

I was standing by the great main gate to my June grass meadow, hoping to guide them to the pasture of my choice. The geese, all twenty-seven of them, followed.

June grass is a most beautiful color of rosy quince at this time of year. The field is covered with it, wild strawberries and clover beneath its canopy. The sheep's fleeces assumed a rose cast. They followed me as I led them to the center of the pasture and sat on a blue-gray lichen-covered rock. Some came close, surrounding me, others wandered off. I sat for a while watching the sky, the sheep, and the ripples made in the rose-colored June grass.

A day or two before, the haymow of my barn collapsed. It was filled with a winter's worth of food for the sheep. A beam broke and 1,850 bales of hay crashed down upon the sheep. All ninety-one of them, blocking their exits along with the goats and two of the cows, were caught underneath, trapped by broken beams and floorboards, bales of hay and shards of wood.

A series of incidents, small and large, had compromised the barn and all who lived within it. A gate placed in order to keep them from danger had trapped them. A gate placed to keep them out had let them in. With the exception of Lady Francesca Cavendish, all of my livestock was trapped inside. It was she alone who remained outside of the barn.

I came home on Friday from a trip to the village only to find hundreds of bales of hay spilling out onto the barnyard. The front wall of the barn was missing two thirds of its face.

I ran around to the north side door and went in. There were five sheep trapped in a corner. And the floor of the mow was down. All I could see was hay, beams, and broken wood. And those five sheep. Staring. The barn swallows were silent. There was not a sound. All was absolutely still. I was certain all the rest of them were dead. Two or three, in my now hazy memory of what I saw, seemed to be in the aisle, but I am no longer certain. There was no possible hope that I could free the five trapped by beams and a collapsed wall by myself.

I ran to the house and called everyone I could think of up and down the creek. I never told anyone who I was. I simply shouted, "Please come if you can. My mow collapsed with 1,850 bales of hay in it. My flock is trapped inside," and hung up the phone. I called the Sheriff's Office, which called the Fire Department, and the great whistle went off in Delhi. What happened next is housed in my mind like images on a Polaroid, fading in and fading out, and in the sounds of men's voices. A laughing one saying where is everybody. A worried one saying this is dangerous. Colors and blurred edges. Sounds. Voices. And the sight of the first sheep coming out. I called them by their own names and by sweet names. And they kept coming out, but not enough of them. I ran to the south side. The firemen had pulled out bales from a corner that had few intact boards remaining. They made a tunnel from which more came on through. I ran back to the north side. More sheep kept coming out. Some stayed close to me, looking deep into my face. Others went to the corn that was on the ground. I heard someone say they're all out. My knees went out from under me. I held on to the door and started to slide down it. I don't want to faint when the Fire Department is here, I thought, and let myself down slowly, grateful no one was around at that moment to see me. I had been so terribly frightened.

People left more quietly than they came. I barely had time to reach out and thank them. Before I had turned around, several others had slipped away. And then more suddenly than it all had happened, I found myself alone with two good friends, my flock and herd and dogs. As if anyone could be alone with two good friends, a flock, a herd, and dogs.

I have had some very hard times in my life. And during each one people have said to me, "It could have been worse." Those words never brought me comfort. Until now. Standing, looking at a simple clearcut disaster, I knew from the deepest part of my soul that it could have been worse. That it wasn't was an equally simple and clearcut miracle. Had I lost my life I wouldn't be knowing it right now. Had I lost but a single animal I would be feeling it forever. No one died. My beloved barn, home of the best part of my life in the winters, has been ravaged. But the remaining three sides stand a proud testimony to the men who built her. The corresponding wall can be a pattern with which to reconstruct the one now lying on the ground. I've listened carefully to suggestions and am accepting some innovations and sound advice. Good friends have come through with help and offers of help. Some sheep have become a little bit clingy, and I am aware of the same need in me. Or perhaps they are simply reassuring me and I don't understand.

The barn shall be rebuilt. We shall be housed for the winter. I still can't begin to know how it shall happen, but it shall. Over and over again I go inside and look at the ceiling that collapsed on my flock. I go closer to the damaged ceiling each time. Today I even reached out my hand and touched a broken stanchion. There will be a moment when I will help to move it all away. Oh, it could have been worse. Much worse. And for that, I am deeply grateful.

FIONA MACDONALD

T HIS IS the first morning I can remember in a very long time that I've woken up feeling in my heart that life is possible. I don't know if it is because Fiona MacDonald has turned up or because of the kindness of friends about the barn or because the weight sitting on my chest for so long has felt its purpose and has finally been outlived. The joy I've always known that keeps one here and lifts each burden has returned. The day is spelled out with its own version of glory and stands before me, crystal clear. For the past few months a cloud had obscured my vision and erased intent from my vocabulary. Where I once used always to do two things at once, I had begun to do only one. Or more often half of one. Yesterday, to compensate for the past two months, I did three things. At once. It can be possible, although even I found it hard to eat lunch (bread and butter) while carrying grain to the chickens and water to the cow. But three things at once it had to be if I am to make up for the stretch of spring and early summer when hardly anything was accomplished at all. Something for the mind. Something for the body. Something for the soul.

Fiona MacDonald turned up, you ask? Wherever was she? Fiona MacDonald has been a joy to me ever since she was born. The first time she broke my heart was when she was but a few days old and disappeared for an entire day. I gave her up as lost to the coyotes, blaming myself for letting her and her mother out too soon. Her mother stared intently at me in the fields. She knew I loved to hold

Fiona and that whenever Fiona was gone for a few minutes it would be because she was in my arms. That night, I found that beautiful creature running in back of my house in front of the carriage house. Alive and well. How she got there or why was beyond my imagination. By one week old she was able to race like the wind and outrun everything on the farm.

A day or two after the barn wall fell and my winter's hay came tumbling down, a new person turned up in the driveway wanting to buy a pet lamb. I tried to sell him one of my tamest young ewe lambs, but his eye caught sight of Fiona. Mark was so persuasive as we stood near the collapsed barn that I convinced myself I could part with her. The argument went that the money was needed for the good of the whole flock and I must be practical. Funny how that argument never works out in the end. Especially the one about practical. So off went Fiona in the big blue truck and I tried not to think about it. I did call, however, the next day to see how she was doing. Fine and taking her bottle, was the reply. The next evening there was a blinking light on the answering machine. I picked up and heard a frantic voice saying, "I've lost the lamb. She's gone!" Fiona had been gentle and docile her first day in her new home. However, when her new owner opened his barn door the next morning she ran like the wind, racing up his driveway, down the road, and back into a neighbor's yard. There she came face to face with a dog, and veering off, raced into a thicket. The woods there had little brush, but the edges of the fields were overgrown. Mark didn't stand a chance. I went with him to look for her but there wasn't a sign. We brought another lamb over, both to lessen Mark's heartbreak over this lamb alone in the woods, there were no farms within easy reach in which she could find refuge, and perhaps to draw her back. The next day I brought her mother to Mark's. Matilda had lamented so loudly on my farm for her lost lamb that I was certain she would call it in. Matilda, however, didn't believe her beloved Fiona could possibly be in this stranger's place and didn't make a peep.

The thing that worried me the most was the behavior of Mark's dog. In the evening, around dusk, its fur would stand on end and it would become alert and menacing, facing a stand of tall trees on one side of the house. I didn't want to tell him, but I thought he had a bobcat in his woods. A few days later, he told me his neighbors had seen a bobcat racing across a field. When he went up to look, it had just killed a fawn.

Every night for the first few days I would wake up thinking about Fiona alone in the woods, her white coat a perfect target for a great horned owl, a bobcat, or a pack of coyotes. As each day passed, hope slipped more agonizingly away, and the wish for her return was replaced by one that her death be a quick one.

In a way, I felt punished for letting her go. I hadn't lost any livestock when the barn wall went down, but because of it I lost Fiona.

In all of this I had ignored who she is. Fiona MacDonald, chaser of pigs. Fiona MacDonald, strategist par excellance. Fiona who has raced her brothers and sisters round and round the big pine trees only to stop short, turn around, and race back into their unsuspecting faces, scattering them everywhere. Fiona MacDonald.

One night, about a week after her disappearance, I came in from the nightly ritual of walking around the flock only to see the red light blinking once more on my answering machine. It was Mark. Fiona had been discovered. He was going to pick her up. The next morning, I was told the whole story. Fiona MacDonald was found on a dairy farm five miles as the crow flies from her last home. Had she taken a reverse turn she would have ended up about here. She was found nursing off a cow and seen eating the farmer's cornmeal supply. She wouldn't let any adult within ten feet of her but allowed the farmer's three-year-old to hold her. She had gotten fat in the wild and at the dairy farm. It took no less than six men to catch her. I offered to buy her back. Mark refused. "No, she's a challenge," he said. I understood.

Fiona MacDonald. Joy of my heart. Outmaneuvering all things wild and hungry. And growing round and tall during the adventure. It is only right that Mark keeps her. But she shall bring me delight forever.

GRATITUDE

THREE JARS of red summer extract sit on the kitchen table. I think I may have gotten the method perfected that preserves this wonderful flavor.

A raspberry bush I've been meaning to cut away at a corner of the carriage house has been giving me a handful a day of berries. And some blackberries have sowed themselves in a ditch cut in a field while we looked for a water line a long time ago. This year, to my astonishment, they've been giving me berries each evening. On a day or two after it rains they are drier but their flavor is more intense. I haven't been on my hill this year, the first time I haven't in the summer since I bought it, but I've heard it was covered in blueberries. This morning I picked sumac from a tree near a wall on my property. The abundance I expected from a stand of it near the road disappeared one day. A tiny insect loves this lemony-flavored pinnacle and devoured all of them. Chokeberry jam and syrup is already made and most of it is bottled. Black currants have yielded their smoky sweetness. The red currants from my garden are now jam. And the elder flowers that I spared are also a syrup, to enhance a glass or two of cold well water after I shovel the barn.

This August was different from all of the others I have ever known. My childhood was spent in hurricane country. Those wild winds, crashing trees, and flooding streets still carried their sounds into all of the Augusts of my life until this one. I have battened down hatches with a frantic attention as if all were dependent upon my efforts. The survival of my family always seemed to be at stake. A rush of sewing late into the night to make school clothes for my children, the frantic pace of knitting needles as I sat on buses or subways, and a mess of pots with food being put up punctuated the days and nights. At times it was as exhilarating as the sounds of the great hurricane winds against the houses I lived in as a child.

My parents made a life for us that was in some way almost stiflingly secure and in another, by act of God, certainly not their own, dangerously insecure. And so in the quietness of the houses where we lived, there was a belief that the storms could not hurt us. And they didn't.

When I first left home and moved to New York City, the winds of the East Coast hurricanes hurled down the narrow streets but without the attendant drama or excitement. Yet as the clear blue skies of summer intensified in August, an occasional sharp crispness in the air warned this Yankee that it was time to get moving, knitting, cooking, preserving, for the winter. Protect and guard the family.

My husband had left the family when the family itself was very young, and he died shortly thereafter. And so while in the early years, or rather moment, of our marriage he was a participant in the act of preserving the family, mostly he stood in absolute amazement at the young hurricane he had married, sweeping through the open-air markets, taking such satisfaction at finding quince or blackberries.

When I came to Greenleaf, I was blessed with an abundance of all I held dear, and I picked and coveted with an abandon held in check only by restraints of time.

I still lived in other places and was a part-time resident for the first ten years of this incredible experience that Delaware County holds for us all. And while frustration also held sway as I often tearfully drove away, much of the abundance that was here found its way to my larder.

This year was a little different. The spring was lost to me in sadness I couldn't shake off, but then the good-humored kindness of the people who stopped their lives to help me took away with them all of the hopelessness that I'd carried with me after the hay mow collapsed in the barn. And left it, I hope, ragged in the ditches to be blown far away on their way home.

It is not that I won't feel worried or frightened or alone again. That would be too much of a demand on my most vulnerable and human heart. But something has altered within me, because of the kindness exhibited toward me and mine this day. And that change will never reverse itself. Last night I walked a mile or so to a friend's house. They were having an end of the summer party. I have known the family for many years. Along the way were sumac and black-berries, ready to pick. The evening air was soft and warm.

Two young members of the family have recently moved into their grandparents' household. I've known them since they were two years old. They are coming one day to pick blueberries high on my hill. I'll tell them to get the sumac on their way over. We will go over the hill and bring down a winter's worth for their grandparents' and my own households.

There is a short time left in which to do this. But I no longer have the sense of desperation and anxiety that has accompanied that race up the hill for me in the past. It shall be a joy to have the girls with me, if they can come. And a joy to have them share the abundance from that high hill. I need to share my gratitude.

BARRED ROCKS

A MAZING HOW interesting a flock of chickens can be, especially to someone who heretofore had been most uninterested in anything whatsoever belonging to the poultry family. I promised myself when I started farming that no matter how delightful the thought of farm-fresh eggs might be, those skinny-legged, cackling, pecking, flustering, hysterical creatures would under no circumstances become part of it. I'd buy my eggs elsewhere, thank you, anywhere else.

These thoughts possessed me as I walked through the rain with a bucket of mash and a can of water down two sets of stone steps, through three wooden gates to the June grass meadow to check on the chickens in the portable chicken coop. With eagerness. What are they doing? Did they lay yet? And if so, which one? And which color? I'd separated the chickens housed all winter in the beautiful and elegant carriage house coop. They are a miscellaneous bunch. Some are of known varieties such as the black sex-linked crosses that I bought on a whim. Others are of the "who'd-ever-refuse-a-pair-of-pullets?" or "my-pet-chicken" or "my-seven-roosters" variety. In other words, breed unidentifiable. They leave under less frequent but similar kinds of circumstances: "Oh, do you have a rooster for my chickens?" And, "Please, missus, I'd like to buy some hens." Or, as in the case of the two sex-linked crosses, captured by my Border Collies, to no good purpose.

The latest group, reputedly heavy layers, are white, albeit they first appeared to be pink after having attacked a black chicken, someone's pet, also in the cage on their way here. They lay white eggs, and have been moved, in a rare successful moment of organization, to the portable chicken coop in East Meadow. There they were joined by the surviving black sex-linked crosses plus one miscellaneous black chicken. The black pet chicken, now recovered, lives with the ducks. The black chickens lay brown eggs. This means that I can tell, of the eleven, which flock are laying what. And more important, how many.

The remaining chickens, housed in the carriage house in a most elegant indoor chicken coop, are some variety of red, russet, brown, buff, with or without black spots. They live with a white chicken that suddenly, a few weeks ago, manifested as a white rooster, as well as a mammoth black, white, and sapphire rooster who has pride of place on the roost and at night.

Those two never fight. Nor do any of my many roosters. The new ones are born here and are gradually accepted or ignored by the great fine dandies who parade around the farm. One developing into a particularly fine specimen of garnet, russet, red, and maroon with flashes of white on his tail, the brother of the all-white one, is leaving shortly to live at a youngster's house as a reward for helping me with barn chores. The others will stay.

New to the farm are some six-week-old Barred Plymouth Rocks (whom I've heard referred to as Barred Rock but I persist in calling Plymouth as well). They seemed to have made an adjustment in perfect safety in with my russet flock, at first. However, one fell victim to my optimism. They were all removed to a separate cage. I'm spending time holding each one in an attempt to tame them. They are very pretty to my eye, and they, as well as their cousins the Plymouth Rocks, may well become my chicken of choice. Chicken of choice? The choice of this sheep farmer who never wanted chickens?

I'd not had a clear perspective of the chickens until now. In the beginning, they were a glorious cacophony of color, sight, and sound, accented by roosters of traditional as well as unusual coloration all fluttering around in the carriage house coop. Tucker, rooster of every childhood storybook with a dark green iridescent tail, was the first to arrive. His harem of five or six accompanied him. They were soon followed by burlap bag upon burlap bag full of roosters, some mustard, buff, cream, and black, others in an imaginable combination of colors reminiscent of the closets of Eastern royalty. Chickens were among them. My flock had begun.

Two young, enthusiastic prospective workers turned up on my farm a short time ago and proved adept at catching and sorting chickens. They are now properly placed in their respective homes. I've made a chart for the wall of my farm office; on it is a series of lists. The first tells how much I feed. The second is divided among the pastured poultry and the chicken-coop poultry with a tally of eggs received each day and their color. I haven't figured out how to size them yet. The third simply totals the day. When I have to buy more grain, I will know exactly how much the eggs have cost.

Of course, the next step is to sell the eggs. But which ones? In my neck of the woods, brown eggs are favored. But some of mine are white. And all of them are different sizes. I've already designed a flyer to give to my neighbors. Mrs. Jorrin's Sheep Farm: Now Selling Eggs. Free Delivery on Thursdays. My Border Collies and I will take eggs up and down the road in a beautiful basket. Perhaps.

Today, in the interest of uniformity, I called my supplier and ordered some of the Barred Plymouth Rocks. Now that the chickens are divided according to color and breeds and I can take an appraising view of them, I've finally made my choice of breed. It is a purely aesthetic choice. The chicken that most suits this farm is the black-and-white breed. To my eye, they are the most chickeny in appearance. Oh, I can already hear the Rhode Island Reds and the Leghorn aficionados' dissenting voices. But no, I've made up my mind. There is a touch of elegance about the speckled black and white, admirably set off by the orange feet and red comb, that appeals to me. They also have brown eggs, of uniform size, to sell after entering the tally of them on long envelopes of thick paper mounted on the wall of my farm office. I am a bit slow when it comes to making decisions on the farm. It is best for me to wait and let the right choice come to me in its own time. And now it has become clear. The Rocks it shall be.

Traffic stopped all last summer on this road, and it will once more. Cars backed up to get the best view of the new structure on my meadows. The structure that moved. The duplex, A-frame, portable chicken coop. "Whatever is that?" I'd be asked by the courageous few who saw me on the lawn. This year, I'm painting it the Charleston green of the wooden fences surrounding the meadows and pastures. Inside, shown to great advantage, shall be the black-and-white chickens with red combs and bright orange feet. Most interesting, at that.

HELPING HANDS

THERE ARE unexpected days that become unsurpassable in a rare combination of beauty and hope. Sometimes without obvious reason. And some, like today, with reasons so simple and clear as to make me fail to understand why they cannot be a regular occurrence.

There has been help on the farm three days in a row. Two young friends have been coming to work for me, bringing another friend along with them. The main thrust of the work has been to clear the debris of the wreckage of the barn, both to assess the true damage and to make clear the way for the man who is going to stabilize the building. It will then be ready for the roof to go on.

In addition to tearing apart and shoveling out and all that it means to arrive at the bare bones of what is salvageable, they have also built a fence that I have needed for many years. Finally, once and for all, I can keep the sheep in or out of the barnyard at my will rather than theirs. Not only will this enable me to confine or release according to my judgment, it will prevent them from interfering with or becoming a hindrance during the reconstruction of their home.

The sheep watched us as the kids pounded fence posts and I picked rocks, repairing the stone wall, making certain all would be straight, and in general fussed around. Three or four sheep watched us with great intensity at our work, commanding attention from me with their penetrating stares. We finished, except for the little spot where I shall put one of my beloved stiles, and I commanded my

Border Collie Steele to "move 'em all out" of the collapsed section of the barn, through the gates, and back into the barn proper.

And so they proceeded to run, contrary to orders, directly toward the stone wall, next to which was the new fence. They scaled four feet of it, and once on top, ran down the wall through the only place it had never occurred to me to block off. So much for the limitations of the human brain. Of course, my excuse was that I have so much more to think of than they do. They have to worry only about how to get past my fences and a few other things some of which I don't pretend to know. I on the other hand . . . I have no real excuse.

My brother is convinced that they were staring so intently at me in order to distract me. I'm not certain of their motive. But I am certain that they did, indeed, distract me.

My new "staff," and I mean that in the original sense of the word, also performed a series of the kind of tasks that produce a visible difference here. I organized their work so that I'd have three quarters of an hour of help from them on some tiny tasks that have remained impossible for me to do but that would make an impact either visually or on my morale.

And so a boulder in the middle of the garden is now gone. My scarlet runner trellis is both installed and secure. My enclosed front porch is now unenclosed. Some rubbish is moved. My outdoor living room shutters have been removed and the views are now unobstructed, and several other minor details that have driven me crazy for quite some time are now corrected. Amazing what extra hands can do! I was then left free to clean the one-room cabin I've lived in all winter in an attempt to make it ready for spring. It even was possible after last night's milking to make some cheese, a few brioche, and a loaf of bread from the whey of the cheese. It was nearly one in the morning when I finally got to bed. But sitting at the end of the day in an almost-well-ordered kitchen, drinking a cup of hot milk laced with sugar and very good vanilla, felt like being fairly close to heaven.

Today, the same sweet crew braved the snow and rain and continued onward to create order from chaos in the barn. There is now nearly enough room for the carpenter to begin. A half a day of work will enable him to reconstruct the framing of the missing south aspect of the barn. I can continue on with most of it myself. Especially since the crew have learned to create neatness as they go along, rather than leaving the cleanup to me. I continue to be impressed. There are piles of wood that can be reused, piles of true scrap, and piles of possible firewood. All in order. The waste hay is neatly divided between bedding and fertilizer. And the floor of the downed haymow is now gone. For all of which I am profoundly grateful.

My days are rarely without incident, and today included a disaster that has been expected for quite some time, though no less of one because it was anticipated. However, I was sandwiched neatly between the valiant work of clearing the barn and a touch of delight that has no measure. And therefore the issue is held between the snowflakes and rain that have fallen all day, waiting to come alive on the first moment that I can address it. The delight is Giuseppe Nunzio Patrick MacGuire. Dale Bryden picked him up today with the truck to have Nunzio's hooves trimmed at Lazy-Ass Farm. It was a great kindness on Dale's part; I had no idea how to find a farrier who knew enough about donkeys to properly do Nunzio's hooves. When Dale and Nunzio came home, Dale had a particular smile on his face that means good news is in the offing. He had tried to work my sweet and handsome donkey after the farrier left, with great success. As I had been promised, but had hardly dared to hope, Nunzio had indeed been trained and knew perfectly well what to do about drawing a cart. He was deemed to be quite nicely trained at that. The news was a pleasure to hear. Soon, my little donkey and I shall be working together to bring order to this farm.

This day is dark and damp and cold. Some of the daffodils have their heads bowed in dismay. But the fire has taken the edge off of the memory of winter. And the kitchen has a welcoming comfortable feeling that reminds me of hopeful times. The colors outside of the windows couple the alizarin crimson of November with the willow green of spring. The rain has caused the grass to become emerald green and the garden is filled with the white and yellow and ivory and orange of the whole family of narcissus and daffodils. The sweet cicely has turned its fernlike elegance into strands of brilliant green. Red-winged blackbirds search for materials for their nests from last year's cicely stalks. How nicely scented must their nests be. A burgeoning order surrounds the outbuilding. Barn and carriage house alike are freeing themselves from the chaos that surrounded them this past year. Sweet cicely approaches them as well. And order begins to emerge from their interiors and surround them once more. Inside the house is a sweetness of comfort and order I haven't known for a long long time. Most welcome indeed.

SHADES OF PEACH AND CORAL

M AY LAMBING has begun. In doing so, it has given me my farm back again. And I have missed it sorely.

Glencora MacCluskie was first. Daughter to Tippy Hedron. And the day before yesterday, a second ewe lamb arrived from a fairly young dam. A chunky fat little thing, round and sweet. No Finn in this lamb but almost all Dorset, with a touch of the Cheviot of her great grandmother's breed.

It has been raining. For days. A north wind creates a damp and chill atmosphere that would be both miserable and disheartening were it not evocative of April. Therefore it is just miserable, not disheartening. I moved the lamb and her mother into the lambing room, unused this year except for pigs. It had been shoveled out and only had debris on the floor that was spilled when passing through, from cleaning out the barn aisle. I started limewashing the walls. After spending a great effort on finding whitewash recipes, I've managed to put together one that doesn't seem to powder and doesn't chip off at all.

In Ireland and some parts of Great Britain, both outside and inside of houses are limewashed. Beautiful colors are made by adding ground stone or pulverized clay or other minerals to the white mixture. A beautiful range of peach and pink is made from adding the terra-cotta-colored raddle that is used to paint on the ram's brisket in order to mark covered ewes to the whitewash mixture.

Each formula I have found included the use of a fat of some sort.

Once I used pork fat, to great success. The latest mixture, from an American formula called Treasury House Whitewash, uses linseed oil as well as spoiled milk. I have some extra milk left over from days when I haven't had time to make my daily cheese, and whey left over from days when I have enough bread and don't need any more whey to make it rise. And there is a quart or two that became contaminated when Francesca Cavendish or Millicent Fallansbee kicked the bucket. Therefore, there is enough to make a limewash paint for the lambing room.

I started applying it on the day I moved the latest lamb inside. Uncertain of how the color would look when it dried, I painted some on an interior wall in shadow and somewhere it could be seen from the doorway when opened. I even tried to measure the proportions of raddle powder, salt, and oil so I could reproduce the color, more or less. What I didn't count on was that different brands of lime would in themselves be different colors, and that the mix using one brand would become pale peach, and a bucket using another would become a muddy drab. Nonetheless, three fourths of a jar of powdered espresso, with the rest filled with coarse salt, plus one and a half gallons of spoiled milk and a half jar of unboiled linseed oil has done it, a pretty pale peach. I'm going to paint the window sashes the same color, the way the Shakers did their buildings, and buy a dark green resin chair to sit in while waiting for lambs to be born. Even partially painted, the lambing room looks absolutely lovely.

Last fall, disaster coupled itself with disaster. I lost some newborn lambs due to avaricious pigs, an experience I hope someday will be erased from the corners of my memory. Madame duVet lost one lamb, as well (not to the pigs), and I bottled her other. Miranda, Tippy, and one or two others also lost lambs to the horror as well. In the flock is a particularly active Finn-Landrace ram. He has been covering ewes with a consistent regularity that surpasses every ram I have ever owned. Even ewes who never freshen out of season have been accepting his advances. Now in the lambing room are a group of very imminent ewes, bagging and bulging, only five and a half or six months away from their last freshening. Gestation is five months. The fact that they are coming in this soon after losing their lambs is remarkable in itself. But even more remarkable is that some of them have never freshened more than once a year. A testimony to a fine ram. Who is not, by the way, one whom I would choose to be this year's flock sire. Nonetheless, flock sire he seems to have become. Every ewe lamb, even the singles born in May of a mother who freshened in the fall, is valuable breeding stock. Tiny shreds of hope for the future of the farm.

This is the time to manage the flock most carefully. The financial future of the farm is completely dependent on the choices I make now. I must be most careful about which ram shall be left with which group of ewes, who shall freshen when, and what I shall have to sell. There are several restaurants that are buying lamb throughout the summer, but I must continue to hold back breeding-stock-quality lambs for my replacements. It is imperative that I keep back more than enough replacements to rebuild a solid flock for the future.

And so, in a deeply familiar movement, I run down to the lambing room five or six times throughout the day to check the latest lamb and the others. I fed them too much grain as a special treat and enough hay to balance it out. Water needs to be carried as well. But I don't mind. I'm refining the space and rethinking what needs to be built for next winter's lambing. By today's end the walls will be limewashed the mottled shades of peachy pink that make everything, including the sheep, look that much softer and prettier. The browns of the mangers become deep and rich. The sheep's fleeces, as grungy as they are at winter's end, have a softer look. The dark green chair will fit in quite nicely. I'll have the men who are putting in a support system in the barn cut me some boards so I can build the shutters I need for the windows. I'll limewash those shutters as well. The sign Jessica Buel made for me a long time ago will be even more outstanding on the peach pink door. And in all ways that most favorite of spaces will serve me even better than before.

The Finn–Landrace sheep from the Cornell flock had been a great disappointment to me. They did not do well, and never, even remotely, came up to the expectations I had for them. However, the young ram, now about two and a half years old, has done some remarkable things. While I can be certain he is father only of lambs that he both has marked and who look like him, I can be certain that every sheep bearing his mark has been covered by him, and in some cases sheep who never off-season lamb have been set into heat by him. Some of those lambs are his gift to the farm. This pretty space, with sheep about to freshen, and one little lamb who at two days old ran up to me and stood ready to be picked up, is beginning to take shape. And that shape is much nicer than it has ever been before.

THE GOOSEBERRY BUSHES

FOR MANY years there have been three gooseberry bushes set on one side of a soft fruit triangle in my vegetable garden. It took me a long time to learn to wait and let them become that particular shade of garnet with ripe quince overtones before picking them. Now some, oval jewels, lie in my freezer waiting for me to prepare the first gooseberry fool of the year. Their leaves look very much like those on the currant bushes, but their stems are characterized by particularly sharp thorns. Picking them requires gloves. But it is well worth it. The particular combination of well-whipped cream and sweet and tart gooseberries is absolute ambrosia.

Yesterday Ernest Westcott and Jim Wilson and I, in Ernest's truck, crossed the bridge at the neighbor's and proceeded to head for the line fence. We had in mind to place another two hundred or so feet of woven wire. Ernest had brought with him some locust posts. I brought Steele and Samantha. Jim brought a willing hand with the fence post maul. We were greeted by the sight of Connelly's men, also working on the line fence. Stringing barbed wire.

Apprehension set in. Immediately. I was greeted with a calm courtesy for which I was deeply grateful. At last it was understood that we were working together for the common good. Or at least my men and I were serious about keeping my sheep in and preventing his cows from getting out. Not that I have ever failed to be serious about it; it just never counted when my sheep got out, no matter how hard I tried.

Tom's foreman told me his men had sighted three of my sheep. Unshorn sheep. The ones who got away when we were shearing. This made my tally of eighty-five right. It was hard to believe I'd been counting incorrectly all of this time. These coupled with two others that escaped shearing made my totals work out. But why hadn't I seen them, and why had they not come home? If the fence I've already installed was keeping them from coming home, then they had to be too young to know the escape route on the upper fields. But where were they?

I spent some time being of minor assistance working on the line fence. I'd vacillated about trying to repair the sheep wall that was so very beautiful and in only minor disarray. Were it fixed I'd save a hundred feet of wire. Were it not to be and I placed woven wire across its face, it stood a chance of being destroyed. I decided to do both. And so I began to relay some of the sheep tip stones as Ernest and Jim cleared brush, readying the wall for woven wire.

It was then that I found it. A large, beautiful, leafed-out gooseberry bush. It was tangled in with something else, but it was a gooseberry bush indeed. They trimmed the unwanted (except by wild turkeys who eat the red berries) barberry and dug up the gooseberries for me.

For a moment, I saw a farm wife standing in front of me in a blue-and-white-checked dress, exacting a rarely sought after price from the men working on her farm. "You must dig that bush for me." Hers was a presence I have neither felt nor seen before. A thin, spare woman, neat in a way I can never be, drying her hands on her apron. The men, silent, freeing the precious find from its entanglement in the stone wall. It came out bare rooted. The woman stood between me and it. And didn't smile. I did. For her, it was too serious a moment. For me, it was something else.

A bit of the Yankee in me awoke for a little while. It would be only half an hour or so before Ernest and Jim would have to address the problem of the swamp they would have to cross and wire. Almost half of a very heavy roll of woven wire was still left. And neither man was wearing boots. I walked back and forth on the property line hoping for a solution.

Crossing through the wire Tom's men had restrung, to get to my side, was no easy task, but I did it. And there, five feet away from the first gooseberry bush, on the opposite side of the wall, were several more, smaller, more easily manageable gooseberry bushes. I dug them as carefully as I could while the farm wife in the blue-and-white-checkered dress reappeared, intently surveying my work. I couldn't get enough dirt around their roots and so, absolutely bare rooted, they went into the back of the truck. The farm wife seemed satisfied and disappeared.

Nearly two hours had passed before I could even think about placing them in the vegetable garden. By then they had wilted. To do something the correct way or to compromise has always been a dilemma for me. I decided I'd put them in the most perfect spots even if the rest of the garden around them wasn't properly prepared. I couldn't do a very good job of the digging, but I did what I could, putting composted pig manure on the top of the dirt and left them, wilted and distraught.

I spent too much time indoors today. My chores were more of the farmer's wife category rather than those of the farmer. It wasn't until afternoon that I began to feel trapped and raced outside to become alive again. I had been told that the bridgeway next door would be closed as soon as they put the cows in.

Steele, Samantha, and I went to see if we had a day or two of grace left to be able to cross it. And it was there that I spotted the three sheep. Small dots in the distance. Keeping the dogs near me I raced across the bridge and up the hill. The sheep disappeared.

Suddenly, as I climbed a rise, I saw one. She ran. The dogs ran. I ran. And they were gone. I walked back toward the pink gate, calling to the sheep I could not see the call that brings them home. It could be only a futile gesture. Not a sign of them anywhere.

The line fence appeared. And there they were. Frantically trying to come home. But now there was a woven wire fence keeping them out. The fence that was to keep them in. They tried the pink gate. It was closed. They ran the line fence, the dogs closely after them. Running through the swamp, two made it through the barbed wire. One became mired. Her fleece was too thick. The two others, seeing she was trapped, came back to her; they had to be too young to know how to get home without her. Grateful that I wasn't wearing boots to slow me down, I managed to open the pink gate. The young ones broke free from the swamp and ran through the gate. Home. I went back to rescue the mired ewe. Connelly's cows suddenly manifested between me and the swamp. I had to go around my woven wire fence again and see if I could reach her from my side.

Of course, when I got there there was no sheep to be found. In my barnyard, having leaped the fence surrounding it, were two very muddy, very wet sheep. One let me hold her. She had always been wary of me, standing behind her dam when I'd come into the carriage house where she lived as a lamb. Her mother was young, nursing twins, and I kept them separate to feed her extra grain. An hour or two later the third ewe appeared, wet and exhausted. She, too, let me pet her. "What took you so long to bring them home?" I said. It had been raining intermittently all day. We were soaked. I went back in the house. The gooseberry bushes were wet as well. Their leaves were no longer wilted and forlorn but rather alert and gleaming. They had taken.

COMPROMISE

I N   T H E   never-ending debate between the right way and the wrong way in which to do things on this farm, very often a compromise becomes the only choice. Yet compromises here are almost always a mistake. While expediency can sometimes be a successful choice in the rest of the world, on a farm, what is expedient most often necessitates returning and doing it all over. On the other hand, how does one decide or have the courage to say no to a load of hay, as an example, that is about to be dumped on some old moldy hay left from the year before, on a floor that had been rained on, through a now-repaired hole in the roof?

Last year I tried to say no but was sufficiently ambivalent that I allowed myself to be persuaded against my better judgment. And while I was profoundly grateful for the hay, I always believed I had made a very big mistake. This year is different. My resolve improves in the fullness of time, and there have either been too many different experiences, or the beginning of some better experiences, that have strengthened it. There will be more animals than ever this winter. I am keeping back at least seventeen lambs as both replacements and additions to the flock. The hay, therefore, must be the best I can buy and the feeders must be the most efficient. The entire feeding operation must take as little time as possible, and I must be able to have more control and less waste than ever. What this means, in part, is that a great deal of construction shall have to be in place before the hay begins to be delivered.

In one of my reprints of old farm books, I have found a picture of what was thought to be an ideal sheep barn. Loose hay was fed out in those days, both lighter and in some ways easier to handle. Part of the mow floor consisted of what is in effect a trapdoor on hinges with a weighted pulley system on the nonhinged side. Hay was tossed onto this trapdoor. When the weight of the hay exceeded the weight on the end of the pulley, the door slid open and the hay slid into the feeders below. The trapdoor itself formed part of the short chute that carried the hay to the feeder. The feeders are situated and built to accommodate the angle of the trapdoor-cum-chute, and the sheep can easily eat from it.

I want this trapdoor in the floor of my barn. Badly, very badly. I had hoped to have it last year. But the sudden arrival of hay, and a lot of it, prevented me from having it built in time. And so I allowed a compromise that was in essence the absolute wrong way to put the hay in the barn. This year, I am determined to put nothing whatsoever in that section of the barn until the door has been installed. The recently installed barn floor is also begging to have some extra posts put in to help support it. That too must be done before the hay goes in. If I were truly courageous, which I am not, I would not allow the hay to go in until those posts had been installed.

A small amount of hay arrived by a circuitous route today. It was unexpected but came in small enough increments to make it manageable. I shoveled and raked and hauled and spread much of the damp and spoiled hay that had matted onto the upper level of the floor, outside. Most of it was sent, to my intense satisfaction, to places that it best served. I was pleased. The little bits of hay that escaped lay on a relatively clean floor and could be raked out onto the mow. No waste here. It also became far more easy to walk, carrying bales to throw over the mow, when the floor was unencumbered by wads of hay clumped together.

Some of the matted hay went to a section of the barn that is about to be shoveled out. Some went over the bridgeway. And some went onto the pasture where the donkey now lives. With any luck, the seeds will be pushed into the earth by his feet, and the manure from the sheep that got mixed in from their occasional visits to the loft will fertilize the ground and the hay scraps will mulch it all to bring back a little grass. I planted some tomato plants yesterday and today. There are a few more left to do. I also planted some radishes and radicchio, both to sell and to have for the house. Rather than waiting until I had properly prepared the entire vegetable garden, I prepared several beds as perfectly as I possibly could and planted in those. I even managed to get the rows relatively straight. The seedlings had come from Georgia, are relatively inexpensive, and are of special varieties that I have not been able to locate in garden centers in this area. It shall be a task to keep the roosters out of the mulch. I love best to use a mixture of sheep manure and chopped hay. The roosters think it makes a great place to take a dust bath. In effect, what the mixture does is provide a source of a slow-release fertilizer each time it rains. By the second year it has disintegrated well enough to lighten the soil and make it far more friable.

While the twelve small, rectangular beds that are left unplanted are in stages ranging from absolutely overgrown to in need of a quick raking, those three well-planted little stone-edged plots have all afforded me guiltless satisfaction. The remaining plots bear no reproach, as yet, because the very correct neat ones are simply offering promise, examples of the absence of compromise.

A clear section of hayloft floor and the well-ordered garden plots gave me somewhat of a change in perspective. I began to view some other little space in the environment with fresh eyes. The yard where the geese are fattened became a source of interest. The manure and bedding had become packed so firmly that barely a blade of grass has had the courage to break its surface. It is fenced to about four feet with chicken wire, a fertilized, fairly sunny spot next to the barn bridgeway.

For several years I've wanted to grow kale to add to the diet of my sheep. I even have some two-year-old seeds. The fenced-off area is next to the barn. It can be easily cut and fed with relative ease, only a few feet from the barnyard. I took a pick and dug a small trench. Sure enough, beneath the concretelike texture of the goose droppings, matted hay, and seven-month-old mixture was some of the blackest, richest soil I'd ever seen on the farm. I immediately thought of planting beans there as well.

Tomorrow I shall watch the sun to see if there is enough to support a garden in that spot. And if there is, I'll plant beans, interplanted with kale. The absolutely right way. Not only shall the nitrogen from the beans support the kale, the beans will be pulled long before their canopy stresses the kale. What is amazing is how doing something without compromise leads to still more solutions. Correct ones.

A PACK OF COYOTES

A PREGNANT EWE was killed by a pack of coyotes the other night on my farm. I didn't hear a sound. The horror of it lingers with me. My farm has been severely menaced by coyotes since spring. They have been bringing my lambs to their pups and feasting on my sheep. I called the Department of Conservation and a conservation officer was dispatched to the farm. Contrary to public opinion, here, at least, no reimbursement is offered for sheep killed by coyotes. The officers themselves can do nothing except make recommendations. They suggested I hire a trapper and offered me the name of one with a sound reputation. For the past several mornings he has been coming to set and reset a series of traps around the farm. The elusive coyotes avoided them. An innocent sheep did not. I've lost fourteen lambs to date, plus two ewes, to two- and four-legged dogs. It is all too heartbreaking.

We are in the midst of a drought, and the sheep have been eating hay for about a week now. The cows stand in the evening, their chins resting on a gate, waiting for a bale to be brought to them. Today, I shall bring them hay in the morning as well. The sheep get some at night, but I shall begin to morning-feed them also. Winter hay fed out in summer.

This was the drought I never believed would happen. The third in four years, a nearly impossible sequence. I remember the first drought. It was a glorious summer, clear and beautiful. The summer people were raving about what wonderful weather it was.

I walked up to Tom Connelly's hill often that year, to get my sheep and bring them home. The incongruity of the absolute beauty of the countryside and the impending disaster, resulting from the summer use of the winter's hay, was constantly on my mind. I knew the year's profits would be lost, fed out on those beautiful sunny days. The winter seemed so far away and yet was ever-present. No matter how hard I was to work that next winter, no matter how many lambs would be born and no matter how many would survive, the profits of it were all burning under my feet. And I knew it. Walking up that pretty, pretty path on those lovely summer's days to Connelly's hilltop to bring my sheep down to parched pastures said it all to me.

A wind blows across the page as I write these words, and the sudden sound of rain accompanies it. I leave the windows open to feel the rain rushing in. The unvarnished floor changes color and becomes suddenly beautiful. The roof in my dining room has begun to leak. And I don't care. The sound above my head is childhood and summer and gratitude all rolled into one. Rain. We have had some whispers of it for a day or two. An hour of a haze so thick it almost could be called rain. And last evening for a quarter of an hour before dusk there was a touch of something so gentle it could hardly be called anything at all. Rainbow weather without the rainbow. But this is the first occurrence in six weeks that could be called rain. Hard, solid drops, straight from the sky, with wind and noise. A gray light between the house and the hills. Thunder. Tree leaves rustling. A faint chill in between the waves of heat.

Between the intimations of rain we've had for the past couple of days, and the sudden effort being made as I write, there is new hope for the meadows and pastures. It is too late for the cows, at least until autumn. The grass will not recover fast enough for them, even if the rains persist on a more normal course, but it's not too late for the sheep by any means. An hour after Nature's gesture, yesterday's clover darkened in intensity and became green again. I shall still see my winter's hay fed out this summer, however; it is a long way from autumn. I still shall see the profit from my winter's labor lying on the summer's earth wasted around the feeders. But we are still alive. At least most of us. Whoever as has not been killed by coyotes.

Last winter I believed there was a possibility I might get killed here. It comes as a shock to me. I feel so alive today. So alive that it comes as something of a shock to realize that last winter I believed I would die. Here. On my farm. The words, "My way of life could kill me," kept running through my mind. Some people's way of life, smoking, drinking, driving carelessly holds the possibility of killing them. Mine is the country. Fresh air. Pink cheeks. Exercise. On a farm, living as farmer. I thought my chances of survival were fifty-fifty. Well, maybe sixty-forty. And I went through the process of accepting it. Every day. Wet firewood. Forty degrees indoors. A dangerous barn. Restless cows. Never enough to eat. I may die today, I thought at least once every day. Because of my way of life.

The rain has stopped again, but a fierce wind blows low to the ground. My son is here to help me, and Don Roberts is addressing the leaks in the house roof. Things are moving very fast all of a sudden and for the better. I've begun to drive myself. A little faster. A little harder. I'm not afraid of the winter this year, no more than I am afraid of the drought. Nor much of anything.

I went up the side hill with the trapper yesterday in order to see where he set traps to catch the coyotes. He is a careful man, deliberate and intelligent. I hadn't said whether or not I wanted to see the dead pregnant ewe. She was one of my firstborn Dorset girls. He went on a bit ahead of me. "Don't come any farther," he said. "You don't want to see it." I didn't. The coyotes had killed it and didn't eat it. The birds had gotten to it some.

I've watched the profit from the farm spilled onto the ground during a summer's drought. I've seen the winter's hay fed out and the lifeblood of the farm spilled out on the ground by coyotes on the attack. I've seen the summer's most beautiful days spell hardship for us all.

MANGEL-WÜRZELS, ROUGE VIF
D'ETAMPES PUMPKINS, AND LEEKS

T HE SEARCH for information on planting the root crop
mangels, sometimes called mangel-würzels, and subdivided
into classifications called Mammoth Red and Golden Tankard, has
led me across an ocean as well as caused me to write numerous letters
and badger countless extension agents. It was to my great joy that I
found, at last, two shepherds at the Royal Agricultural Show in
England who fed mangel-würzels to their sheep. They gave me
planting information and argued between themselves, to my edifica-
tion and education, about the relative merits of each type.

This morning's mail brought me a fall catalog from Smith and
Hawkin. I'd bought a pair of barn shoes from them once but nothing
else; they are a bit too precious for this farm. The covers are too
pretty, however, for me to tell them to stop sending the catalog. As I
looked through it, hopefully, finding nothing to covet, suddenly
there it was. The barn thermometer of my wildest dreams! With a
picture from a French seed packet of a smiling Gallic farmer, red
cheeked, stout, holding a formidable mangel under each arm. The
Mammoth Red under the right and a Golden Tankard under the
left. I want that thermometer. And I want those seeds. Having
tracked them down across this continent and the adjacent ocean, the
mangels have come to me. It has taken too long. I've wanted and
needed to extend my ability to feed my stock for a very long time
now. I've deliberated about planting Jerusalem artichokes and

mangels and kale for a number of years. My whole-farm planner, Dan Flaherty, has tried to shy me away from annuals, and while I understand that, it is tempting to try anyway.

For what seems like eons, I've wanted a farm stand as well. This year, my tomato investment died because I had to earn some mortgage money away from home and couldn't keep up with the watering. The leeks survived, however, and are beginning to look good. I don't want to sell them all, though, as they are almost all that I have from the garden. But hope reigns high at the moment, and I am thinking once more of what to plant next year.

It is barn-shoveling time now, and I'm going to have to put it all somewhere. Why not move it a little farther in the pasture and pile it on an ideal section of field to begin to decompose? I've also wanted to do the big fluted dark orange pumpkins for a very long time. They keep exceptionally well, don't turn to mush when they freeze and thaw, and can be left frozen in the barn and then sliced and fed to the sheep. But where to put them?

I love to walk around this piece of land and think. Unfortunately, it is a slow process. Not the walking. Just the thinking. It seems to take so long to come up with the right solution here. Everywhere I've thought to put the farm stand and the pumpkins has never seemed right. Too far from the road to carry things. Not enough sun. At last, however, the right sites for the farm garden and stand have presented themselves to me. I had unintentionally ruined a corner of pasture by feeding out hay on it for cows. They stomped down the earth and in all other ways compacted and smothered the ground so that absolutely nothing cares to grow on it. It is a corner only a few feet away from the vegetable garden and my house. At the opposite corner of the pasture is a charming spot right outside of the fence, perfect for placing a farm stand. It is next to my driveway and a good pull-off place for cars. The potential garden site has full sun all day, as well. And it won't be taking anything away from the pasture because nothing can grow there at the moment anyway. But piling composed manure there will create favorable soil in that section of the field in the fullness of time. In addition, it isn't too far away to push a wagon or wheelbarrow to the farm stand site.

I have a copy of one of Lee Valley's marvelous reproductions of old farm books. In it are plans for making all manner of structures from tree limbs. I am about to get a supply of elm, some of which would be ideally suited to creating a small stand in which to sell some produce. I've yet to find the correct place to grow the mammoth reds and the golden tankards. They are said to be milk makers. I shall find out soon enough, Along the same fence, bordering the driveway, is the ideal strip in which to grow turnips. It is forty feet wide and about one hundred feet long. Were I to plant the small red-and-white turnips in that spot, I'd be able to move electric net fencing for forty days, one strip of one-foot by one-hundred-feet each day, to feed my sheep. Strip grazing. In the process they would fertilize the ground and pound their manure into the earth with their little sharp feet. It was the realization that root crops could be winter fodder for livestock that revolutionized farming in the Middle Ages. All hay had to be cut by hand and stored in hayricks, subject to the same kind of spoilage that our farmers are now discovering in the use of round bales. Many had to slaughter some livestock in November rather than allow them the possibility of going hungry in the winter. Once root crops began to be fed out, things changed dramatically. Both cows and sheep would eat the tops and pink roots, and the pigs and geese would be fattened on what was left in the ground. I'm going to try it.

For many years, I listened to some sound advice to not spoil my pasture with crops. I'm glad I listened because the places that I had considered were the wrong ones. But this plan and the needs prompting it have evolved slowly, as I believe farming decisions should. For the first time it seems correct.

There are days when life seems possible. That I have a fighting chance. Although, I must admit, I can't remember when I last thought I had one. This chance was given to me by the fact that the apartment in my house is rented. Despite the continuing huge sums that are being demanded of me to refine the place, it means that this month, at least, there's enough money to take care of the house. And suddenly I can be creative about the farm. It is easier to get up in the morning. And pushing a little harder at the end of the day no longer feels like a burden. To go the extra mile for fifteen minutes seems worthwhile.

In the morning I shall call one of the extension agents who have worked very hard to help me demystify the raising of the mangels and tell her about my latest find: the thermometer decorated with Golden Tankards and Mammoth Reds. I'll call Dan Flaherty to ask how to prepare my pasture for next year's turnip crop. The pumpkins shall be familiar enough to do on my own. Henry Kathmann cut down an elm for me today. Some of the wood might become part of the farm stand. I may even start drawing ideas for the sign. It would be so tempting to do that French farmer, with a mangel under each arm.

PIGS AND COWS

THE LATEST round of Tamworth pigs are due to arrive on Friday. Six of them. I intend to be ready for them. In the absolute. Pigs have been known to cause me, on occasion, great grief. On the other hand, they have earned money and provided the best pork this family has ever eaten. These six pigs are the final experiment. If it doesn't work, there shall be no more pigs.

My old books of plans for sheds and outbuildings and other farm accoutrements show various plans for pig houses. I've found one I like the best and hope to convince Henry Kathmann to spare some time to build it for me. He understands farm-building projects extremely well and indulges me with clever solutions to the complex problems that this farm often presents. There is some green metal left from the roof, a few pieces shortened to size, that will make an admirable roof. And there is some straw that once called itself hay that will bed them. And I have extra wood from the barn-building project, already cut. The latest plan is to make the pigs root up the field that wants to become my truck garden, complete with mangels, kale, turnips, leeks, and tomatoes. This year, after they leave a well-secured place in the barn, the pigs will be enclosed by electric fencing within my wood fencing in the designated sections of pasture. I shall work one third of it this fall. If it proves successful, next spring's pigs will start the second third.

I still see, in my mind's eye, a well-functioning, well-integrated farm, all components relating well with each other. Although the dream of it became a bit tarnished for a while, it is beginning to come alive again. Nunzio, at the muck cart, has been helping me spread valuable nutrients across the fields, as well as pulling an A-frame sledge in the winters to plow out the driveway. The chickens fertilize my pastures in the portable chicken coop and give me eggs, and their winter litter fertilizes my flowerbeds. (The phlox that had their benefice this year grew to be twice as tall as the ones that didn't.) Next year the geese, inside electric fencing as well, shall do their job of fertilizing and pay by their sacrifice for the grain bill of the sheep. The pig money pays for grain for the sheep as well. The sheep, God bless them, keep my pastures in order, provide manure for the fields and help others start their farms when I sell their composted black gold, and pay for their own hay. In addition, they provide me with a peaceful heart in the calm, still barn that I have never known anywhere else.

The cows must not be overlooked. How could they be? Their calves are designated to pay all notes of obligation on the barn roof restoration. And, in a week or two, some shall go to the CADE Project's pastured veal program. They have been out on pasture all summer, with access to Millicent and Francesca's milk. It has been a drought year; therefore, I do not expect anything impressive in the way of weight gain. However, it was an act of faith to participate in the program, and one needs to do that once in a while.

I must admit, I am as conservative a farmer as could be imagined. Cynicism and skepticism have woven themselves throughout my thinking. Promises and profound hope have given rise to expectations only to let me and other farmers whom I know down so many times that is has become an act of faith to participate in anything that I don't personally control. What I've seen so often is white-collar jobs being created or sustained by the well-meaning at best, self-serving at worst, in order to "assist" the farmer. Nonetheless I've committed two calves to the program, with more hope, obviously, than reservation. And off they soon shall go.

The cows provide me with milk as well as calves, for which I shortly shall be profoundly grateful. A new cow, gift of the pigs, and I leave that one for you to figure out, is due to arrive this weekend. Her calf, if it is a bull, is already spoken for, and her milk shall be most welcome. I've not had fresh milk since putting the extra calves on my cows this spring, a big loss to me in more ways than one. The pigs shall get the benefit of the whey from the daily cheese making.

I shall have fresh butter, cheese, and milk for the cappuccino I used to love in the morning. And if I decide to be completely extravagant, I'll buy a yogurt maker. My house is never consistently warm enough to keep milk attempting to be yogurt at an even temperature. Unless, of course, I can convince Henry Kathmann to make me an old-fashioned hay box, the kind that people used to have to keep yeast-risen dough, or things like yogurt, well insulated and at a steady temperature.

While haying and harvest are both exciting times on a farm, if all goes well, the most exciting time to me is when new animals arrive. I am blessed in that a hundred or so more lambs are born here each year, as well as calves and chicks.

And so to have both the pigs and cow arriving within twenty-four hours is especially exciting, in addition to the awe that a new force, pigs and cows being the most forceful of my livestock, brings here. A new dimension of hope and possibility always accompanies both the anticipation of the arrival and the onset of their stay here. It never really fades, even after we are all settled in with one another. In a way, they take care of me, giving me what I need to have in order to take care of them.

THIS IS A DAY

THIS IS a day the Lord has made. Those words are usually the first that come to my mind each morning when I get up. The words that follow are always more tentative. Sometimes they will be variations on the central theme. And who I am is what I make of it, also occurs to me. There are other variations as well.

When I was seven years old I wrote a story about God. That story integrated Him into my daily life. And by the time I was eight I had decided for certain what His plan was. I decided that He presented us with circumstances, and who we are is what we do with those circumstances. This has been a guiding principle for me ever since. I measure the day accordingly.

The sun has just crested the horizon and lit the walls of the pink room where I sit, one eye looking out of the window to see that the sheep are staying home and that the cows are finding something worth eating. Each day is an opportunity, with themes and variations, to go beyond simple survival and, rather, to live.

There are tasks, inevitably, and here on this farm, at least, too many to be filled in one day. Some tasks are seemingly straightforward. Wash the kitchen floor. Shovel the barn floor. Others are less so. While washing the kitchen floor remind yourself to be more consistent in keeping shoes off in that room and better at mopping spills when they happen. When shoveling the barn concentrate on what being a shepherd really means. To find some joy in the appointed tasks is another requirement. For without joy, what is the point? That is more difficult a thing to do. And that is one of the things that define us to ourselves.

Of all of the many burdens that face the day, what are the ones that I can do something about? That seems like an easy question. But the mind is a tricky thing, and often intrudes, reminding me of problems that have no solution, at least at the moment. I can't pay some bills that are worrying me today. Or even tomorrow. But what I can do is find the address that I've misplaced and send out a story already written, on speculation, to a magazine I haven't written for before. And while sending that out I can know in my heart that action is being taken. I can be firm in my resolve to chip away in increments that which could easily seem overwhelming were it to be done all at once. And I must be clever and understand that some actions must be taken even when seeming unreasonable or frivolous, if only to give my spirits a lift.

Some days are given an all-encompassing directive. Perhaps a command. Make no new messes and clean up one old one. Inside and out. The human heart can carry only just so much. Some messes of the heart must be tidied as much as a mess in the cellar. Some days the directive is more subtle. If there is something you feel badly about, something that burdens your heart, fix it for someone else. If you feel nothing is ever going to happen to you unless you do it, do something unexpected for someone, to lift their spirits.

Some days have a built-in command. Have faith. Believe just for today that the problem repaired must not be diminished by the one still lingering. Translated into practical terms, buy the corn with the money earned by the sale of some lambs that you designated to pay for corn. The mortgage will have to be paid some other way. Don't borrow the mortgage money from the grain money.

I write lists. Wonderful lists. "Greenleaf Demystified" is the title of one such list. It is a master list created to show the family and me that there is not that much to do to make things seem really nice here. It is not that overwhelming. Easily accomplished in units of one or two or three hours. And if those things are done, everything will seem and in fact be so much better.

The lists entitled "Enchanting" and "Toward Enchanting" are ones that most affect the human heart and give joy to the spirit. Some things on them are as practical as a bed. But, oh, what a bed! A copy of a sixteenth-century French box bed to go in the loft of the barn in which to sleep when it becomes impossible to go back to the house in the throes of winter. I've already found the absolutely correct material with which to make curtains for it and a lovely little curved window that had come from somewhere here at Greenleaf a long time ago. It is to have a crown molding around the top and a mattress of barley chaff, if I can get some from Robbie Kathmann, and feather pillows. It shall be enchanting.

"Toward Enchanting" is a slightly lesser list with more practical overtones. At least that's what I thought when writing it, but I may be changing my mind about its designation. Why would I ever designate stenciling dogwood blossoms on my walls "Toward Enchanting" and a shepherd's bed "Enchanting"? I'm not sure. Perhaps it has to do with the degree it can lift the human heart.

I've never known whether to spend a whole week and shovel the barn. Or a whole week to winterize the house. I tend to say that one hour a day committed to a problem will accumulate, and the task will be done. In time.

There are lists and notes in books and on sheets of paper. Some have notes attached saying if I spend two hours a day on "Out of Control" and two on "Greenleaf Demystified" and of course something on "Enchanting," I'll probably be finished by such and such a date. Believing that the day is defined by what I do with it becomes a burden in itself. On a farm, a lot occurs because of what someone or something else has done. While writing this I've gone outside twice because the sheep have moved away from my line of vision. The second time they had, indeed, gone through a hole in the stone wall, to breakfast at Connelly's. The 330 feet of woven wire I put in a week or so ago are still standing. They just found an alternative route.

Tasks of the day are not only practical. They involve our obligations to people as well. And those burdens can be the heaviest of all. Each day also presents an opportunity to give love. I've always thought that if there were something you believed you needed, that created an obligation to give someone else that very thing, someone whose needs are greater than yours. And so there are some additional things to do today, or rather, an additional list to make. For today, that list shall include writing two letters, not of amends or obligation but to bring a touch of the unexpected, a surprise, a feeling that one never knows what this day shall bring into two lives. Lives of people I care very much about. For this is a day the Lord has made.

BUSMAN'S HOLIDAY

S ATURDAY WAS a very special day for me. It was the one day a year that I consider to be my day off. Of course, that included getting up at five a.m. to get enough of my chores done so that someone could reasonably take over for me. Nonetheless, it was truly a day off.

I spent the day at the New York State Bred Ewe Sale and Show in Rhinebeck. A busman's holiday, of sorts. This was my fourth year visiting this show, and I loved every minute of it. There are wonderful sheep to look at from all over the East Coast, breeds I rarely see anywhere else. Some I covet and some I simply admire. There are incredible books about everything one needs to know about dying wool and knitting and, yes, raising sheep. The yarn choices are beautiful, although I must admit my favorites always come from RipRap Farm in Windham. All others pale before her angora-and-wool blends. I ordered the most amazing color, a cross between raspberry and garnet, to be dyed for me. I am to make a special sweater from it. It had suddenly occurred to me that I'd like to wear something nice for Christmas, rather than looking like I slept in my clothes when I come downstairs Christmas morning. This fair does that to me. It is inspirational. It makes me remember that life can have its graceful moments. Especially after looking at these lovely yarns. And, in fact, the fair itself is a graceful moment in a shepherd's life.

My daughter and several of our friends all meet one day at the fair. Justina and I have a passion for the homemade ice cream, the world's second-best ice cream, served in homemade waffle cones. We debate about when in the day we shall visit the ice cream stand. I opt for eleven A.M., before lunch, and am outvoted every time. Once I even had two cones, one in the morning and one in the afternoon. The lunchtime food is acceptable if not wonderful, the meatballs are good. The elephant ears are the best. They are our grand finale. The sheepdog trials are beautiful and make me love my dog Steele even more.

What this fair does for me as well is to delineate the year. My involvement with the flock and lambing begins to accelerate after the fair. This year I am in a far more hopeful state than I had any right to be in last year. It was about this time last October that I came to understand that the amount of money raised by the fund to restore my barn was unlikely to grow in any significant manner. There had been enough hay in the barn, but by October most of it was still on the ground. The roofer had begun to play bird in the hand, bird in the bush games with me. I was his bird in the hand, so he could court other birds in the bush and keep me waiting. I was never certain that he would install my roof. I didn't have enough firewood that was dry and didn't have enough that was green, either. I went to the fair looking for hope and inspiration last year. It was there, but the winter proved to be an endurance test. This year has been much better. It is as if I've been wielding a massive sledgehammer on all that is formidable here, swinging it with a consistency that has been unusual for me. Bashing down all things that have stood in the way of order and peace of mind.

I am only a few days away from seriously addressing the barn again. Those few days include the livestock, however. The geese must be put in for the duration. Their duration. And last year's pen needs be redone in such a way that it functions. There shall be a new gate built into it so I can water and feed them easier and so grain trucks can bring me what I need nearer to the grain chute, relieving me of the necessity of carrying fifty-pound sacks up the barn bridgeway and down a flight of stairs. By this time next week the geese should be properly inside and the pigs properly outside.

A neighbor is going to help me build a pigpen in the south pasture so the pigs can root up a field where I shall plant some crops next year. It will create less for me to muck out of the barn and in doing so fertilize the field. It also should be both easier to feed them as well as making life a bit more manageable. Tomorrow I shall finish painting some lengths of fence that have remained unpainted far too long, giving a more finished aspect to Greenleaf for a change. I'm starting to muck out the barn, and for some reason I am optimistic that it shall be done in time even though I've started it late. For the past ten years, I've spent each fall with paper and pencil trying to figure out how to get the best food for my sheep at the best price. This year is no different. And so this morning, the first after my day off, I spent some time with pen and paper, working out grain cost and prices, volumes, and daily feed programs. If I keep the young stock separate, then I can feed them corn, and if I put the rams outside, then I can save fifty cents a day for one hundred and twenty days. In between the colors of corn and molasses floating through my thoughts are visions of a quince-colored yarn I bought to make the barn sweater I designed for my daughter (it took four years of developing one design a year finally to arrive, on the fifth year, at the perfect design) and the colors I am going to mix to make a little sturdy outdoor sweater for a baby I've grown to know and a vest for my new son-in-law.

Here at home are the beeches, the golden ocher I love so well. The russet oaks form a perfect background. The sun breaks through the steel gray clouds for rare moments. The wind blows. And I have not yet made a fire. But somehow it doesn't really matter. What matters are the inspiration and the many choices.

AN AMERICAN SOUP

I LOVE THIS weather. The wind howls, rages, and roars, with an occasional high-pitched whistle, rushing through the open floorboards that are both my porch ceiling and my bathroom floor. The day is damp and gray with winter overtones. And it is an act of triumph to be dressed warmly enough and yet able to commit to barn chores.

I always forget how much I love the cold, until it begins, when I've got a system down, that is. And today, so far, I have. The carriage house is well on its way to achieving some semblance of order, and it becomes even more so by afternoon. I started stacking hay, untangling it from the mass confusion of its summer arrival. *Never again* became almost a chant. Never *what* again is the question. Perhaps never again to be talked into doing something that I don't want to do. I've had the same lesson brought home to me over and over again. What appears to be immediately convenient on this farm is often grossly inconvenient in the long run. The man bringing the hay was in an understandable frenzy to get it under cover. And I yelled, screamed, stamped my foot, and said no in every conceivable way I could, but to no avail. His logic prevailed. The hay was there. Hay in my mow is better than hay in his barn. We all know that to be a fundamental truth.

Unfortunately, an equally fundamental truth is that hay thrown every which way in July will probably stay that way until October. The barn was overloaded too. I regaled my hay man with all of the reasons why he should stop any further delivery. I couldn't stack any more. Alone. "I'll never get it stacked," I cried, tears streaming down my face. As a result, this weekend I shall have to pay my contractor to put a post in to remedy the sagging joist. I couldn't properly stack the rest, and the hay is unbalanced. Nonetheless, the hay is in and I am secretly grateful. I need only another six to eight hundred bales, which shall be delivered weekly, as I had wanted hay to be delivered all along. The anticipated hay is excellent, I've heard, and shall arrive in manageable increments.

There is something so satisfying about stacking hay in brisk cold air, wearing gloves that are not soggy from the heat, and having coveralls that effectively cover all, so no hay pierces one's skin. It was a good feeling to start to restack the cows' hay in the upper level of the carriage house. Half of it is neat and finished and under a mantle of black plastic. The floor is now swept clean. All of the scraps are in the hay chute. Order has successfully claimed this day. I put up a basket in which to keep my gloves, which are frequently misplaced. And I've added a convenient pad and pencil on a string to write down the amounts of hay and grain that I use. Recently a friend gave me some chickens that were about to molt. They now live in the carriage chicken coop next to the nicely stacked hay. No eggs. I don't exactly know how to fatten them, but I'm trying. Five are marked for the pot. However, there has been of late not only the absence of a gas-cooking stove, but the woodstove that has helped me cook has developed a crack and I'm reluctant to use it until it is repaired. However, ingenuity has triumphed. The brisk chill air has demanded something more sustaining than an omelet cooked on a hot plate when coming inside from the wind blasting Greenleaf in the afternoon. (Someone told me there are very few winds that come from the north. He should have been here today.) I couldn't find any of my old iron pots in which I could cook in the fireplace, so I simply wrapped some potatoes in aluminum foil and put them under the ashes in the living room fire. It has been heaven to be able to come in from the barn and pull out beautiful baked potatoes that melt butter instantly. They are perfect. Absolutely perfect.

One night last winter I read a memorable passage from a Georges Simenon book about the redoubtable Inspector Maigret. One in which he went downstairs into a French farmhouse kitchen (Normandy, I'd like to imagine) at four-thirty in the morning. The lord of the manor, and he was a French version of a lord, was eating a bowl of hot soup. The soup had been simmering on the back of a big old coal stove all night. Maigret ladled himself out a bowl and ate, in silence. I imagined that soup to be very, very thick and fairly smooth, with the only real texture from small pieces of fatty ham. Like our slab bacon, in one-inch chunks. Somehow, that soup always has seemed to be a pale orange in my mind's eye. Perhaps it's been colored by a few carrots, so the soup is not too sweet, and by the orange rutabagas of my childhood (I hated them) that my mother used as the obligatory yellow vegetable so often in the winter. I'm not certain I'd even like that soup. The Norman French don't use much garlic. But I wanted that soup. Here, in the morning. Eaten in silence without a word to the dogs. Before going outside.

Yesterday I made such soup. Neither yellow nor orange, but brown, green, and red. An American soup. Soldier beans. Slab bacon. Bay leaves. Tomatoes. Garlic. Kale. It takes well to a slow simmer on a hot plate. This morning it seemed suitable and fitting, on this nasty day, to have it for breakfast. Wonder of wonders! It fueled me for an entire day. Maigret's farmer knew something. And someday I shall try to recreate that soup, soup that was described as a feeling with no mention of a single ingredient. I just know of what it had to be made.

One of the most satisfying things about farming is achieving a sense of order. When everything is in its place, and everyone has been fed, and all is as well as can be expected, there is a feeling like no other. Secure for the moment. But I rarely achieve that feeling for myself. Coming inside the house often means confronting tasks undone, preparations not made, a life unsecured. I farm alone, in a manner of speaking. Although it doesn't exactly seem that way when, on occasion, there are people here to put up a fence, or put the barn back on the sill, or bring me my supplies. And it's equally hard to view myself as alone with Steele, Samantha, and a substantial number of animals around me all of the time. Nonetheless, there is no one but me to make the house comfortable to come into after or in between chores. I'm beginning to miss having a stove in which to bake apple tarts or Shaker Daily Loaves, or Prune and Walnut Rye bread for that matter. It is now dark. I've drawn what curtains are hanging and wonder when I'll get to sew, iron, or hang the rest. I brought in some sticks of pine for the fire, old and dry. The living room smells of them burning. My leather work gloves are a still life on the coffee table, next to a plate of apples I fished out of the brook the other day when I went to check the new line fence. My coffee is nearly hot. The American soup bubbles on the burner. For the moment, at least, all is well.

THE NEW STOVE

THIS HAS been a curious day, to say the least. A friend gave me a very antique cast-iron wood-burning stove for which he had no use. It arrived last evening. Don Roberts, contractor and gentleman, brought it with his men and proceeded not only to take apart and move my original one but also to set up the "new" one and wait until it began to throw off enough heat to ensure that it was working properly. I was initially reluctant to burn very much in it, until I saw what it could and couldn't do, and so I spent the evening in front of the living room fire. Freezing.

For some reason I don't exactly understand, my trusted fireplace has not been doing its proper job this year. The temperature of the house was perhaps forty degrees. And I, tucked in a chair lined in both a deerskin and a lambskin, wearing three sweaters, found myself attacked by waves of chills. I know I'm in big trouble when, in such predicaments, my mind steps in and begins to analyze the situation. I begin to try to remember my nursing school physiology. What causes chills, exactly, I ask myself. How many minutes or seconds elapse between each wave? Why do they start in my back when that is against the deerskin? Et cetera. Et cetera. Big trouble. I then begin to think about people in Bosnia in the winter. Very big trouble. I then feel guilty about complaining.

This morning I lit the new stove, and to my amazement the room became twenty degrees warmer in less than half an hour. I can live with this, I thought, while running around the house synchronizing the two thermometers and trying experiments to see if heat really does rise, or does it expand, or does it push aside the colder air in the rooms above the now overheated kitchen. Exactly what does it do? And how long does it take to do it? And how, ultimately, does it work?

What I think now is that my beautiful, expensive, Danish enamel stove did not ever do its proper job. This antique black cast-iron stove has thrown out more heat in less time with less wood than the stove I have depended on to care for me for the past twenty years ever even insinuated it could.

By the second hour of being warm, my mind began to become less obsessed with being cold and, while somewhat obsessed with being warm, could also think of other things. Wonderful what a little heat in the house can do to one's creativity.

It became unbelievably simple finally to finish turning my yellow studio into a well-functioning room. The beautiful desk that Ernest Westcott built and Don Roberts managed up the stairs (it was, of course, a mere one inch too big all around to get through any of the doorways) and into the former servant's bedroom is now gleaming with old maple finish and well balanced on its extra-long lilac tree legs. It has been positioned and repositioned precisely until it now affords me a view of my sheep and cows from the windows overlooking the barn and barnyard. There is a very nice wooden box with fax paper and foolscap on which to write underneath it, and my little antique French inkwell is filled. The desk is five and a half feet long and almost three feet wide. I shall learn to sort and file and keep track of my life on it.

Even more amazing is what a little heat in the house can inspire. The room is closer to what it needs to be than it has been in a long time. I lack only a lady's slipper chair in which to sit and look out onto the flock. My own little chair had been sacrificed to serve in the little third-floor library. But another shall surely fall in place from an auction or sale. The servant's bed, narrow and neat, has been a daybed and is now my winter bed. The indoor one. I intend to have another one built for the loft level of the barn this winter. My closet is now perfectly arranged with sewing and knitting things. It is amazing to me the freedom that comes with so small a degree of what we take for granted in our lives. To be warm enough. Not to get a shock of cold when going from one room to another.

What that shock does to one's mind is amazing. I found myself, the other day, wondering how many other people have felt this same incredible narrowing of the perimeters of their lives. How many are there in the world even now, as I sit here, unable to concentrate because they are cold? There are countries at war and others at peace whose people face the autumn and the winter knowing that their very minds will soon not belong to them but become the possession of the cold. I console myself with knowing that most people have lived this way since time began and human beings moved farther and farther north. But they learned over generations how to survive in it, I think. It is left to me, however, once more to reinvent the wheel. It becomes an interesting obsession, being cold, viewed with some detachment and some fear. And now, in a room that has on occasion today, verged on more than warm enough, it becomes a revelation to realize what the mind is capable of, unfettered.

The sheep have begun to draw me to the barn more and more often these past few days. They offer me so much peace and comfort at the onset of winter. They replace my thoughts with a silence that is almost impenetrable. One moment at a time an accord is reestablished. And a sense of rightness pervades my time there. With the grace of God it will be nearly as well within this house. It can never be the same. It will always be different. The house houses my mind. The barn, my heart.

ONE FARMER'S DAY

THE CALF that has been named but is not yet called by his name has been finding a way out every day this week. He is a red Jersey. It is hunting season. Aside from the fact that I don't want him out, I have been afraid for him. So it is with a sigh of relief and a measure of satisfaction that this morning I found him in the carriage house exploring the place where the cow grain is stored. He isn't yet sure what grain is all about, but it seemed to interest him. It was a simple thing to get him into a cow stall. One semiskilled maneuver and he was in. The problem of how to confine him, particularly alone, had been on my mind for a while.

My cows, Lady Francesca Cavendish and Dame Millicent Follansbee, have learned their place and haven't tried to move beyond the pasture and onto the lawn to graze for quite some time. And I have, as a direct result of their disinterest in the lawn, become lax when drawing the gate shut. So it was with a modicum of surprise that I greeted both of them not simply outside of the pasture but on the back lawn trying to push open the door to the carriage house. This was too good to be true. I've wanted them in as well. It is time to begin a winter feeding schedule, and the mornings have been twenty degrees by seven o'clock, a bit cold for them to be lying on the damp ground, especially as Francesca is springing and Millicent is still nursing. I swung open the stanchion gate and in they came.

I've been working on making sense out of the carriage house for the past few weeks. The top of the two stories is nearly neat. Spare chairs are hanging from pegs, as are spare cages. Some of the hay is stacked and in order. The floor is swept. The sweepings of hay have been transformed into fresh, sweet-smelling nests for the chickens. The sweepings from the area surrounding the chicken coop have now been put in a flowerbed. The phlox top-dressed with last year's leavings were glorious this year.

Cat food is in a very nice metal can from last year's popcorn with a picture of an idealized farmstead on it. In blue, no less. The kittens have an acceptable feed dish and a fine water dish. The moment one of them notices I have arrived, they rush out of a tent they seem to have made for themselves from a crevice between three hay bales. I hope I don't move those bales in a moment of forgetfulness.

Five new Barred Plymouth Rock chickens arrived this morning and are now ensconced in the carriage house. They are fine hens and I am delighted to have them. My little Barred Rock pullets haven't even thought about laying yet, but I love them. I do still expect great things from them. These new hens are, however, a handsome addition to the flock. The rooster that accompanied them has been joined by other roosters. A fine fellow he is! He got attacked by one of my Banty cross roosters while still in his cage and had to be set free, the better to defend himself, before I was quite ready to put him out. He shall live with the others for a while until I am ready to put him with this flock. With any luck I might get some Barred Rock chicks.

The pigs have a run in the barn aisle now, which I have hopes shall become well rooted up. I suspect, however, they won't find it interesting enough to help me dig. I fed out some hominy to them because cornmeal wasn't available the last time I went to the village. They don't seem to like it. Too much was left in their feeders today, so I strew whole corn in the aisle, but that generated more interest from the sheep, well walled away from the aisle, than the pigs.

I've lists of things to do hanging in every conceivable place that needs me to have a reminder. And I did not do a single thing on them today. Or rather, not in the way any of it was entered on the lists. When I wrote "clean the carriage house for one hour" I didn't mean the loft and I didn't mean sweep every stem of hay into the hay drop for the cows. I meant the downstairs that constantly rearranges itself without any direction from me.

Instead of obeying lists I went where the call was the most compelling. And that took me to the unbalanced hayloft, which is beginning to sag. It is in trouble and has already kicked the barn out in a corner off its sill on the good side, the newly roofed, newly floored side. I do best walking on hay, particularly on hay bales turned every which way, in my stocking feet, so off went my boots, and to my surprise they landed next to the shoes I wear to town. When did I take them off in the barn and why? Up the hay bales I climbed. I wasn't stacking, just throwing them over onto the center aisle floor. And suddenly, more than enough was moved.

The midlevel of the barn has been on the chaotic side of order or, rather, disorder since all of the fleeces were piled on a table in there last May and since hay arrived and spilled through the doorway in July. It symbolized being out of control to me. Fleeces dripping off a table, hay spilled everywhere, obscuring whatever is underneath it, chaos personified. And so I took a broom and rake to it. Per usual, it was far less involving than one would expect.

With a small amount of effort, and a little bit of time, the floor became swept clean, and the geese penned immediately outside of its great door became bedded once again in dry hay. Amazing how wet geese manage to make their home. Ernest Westcott put a new handle on the door to the loft, as well as a spring on the door to the goose pen. I can now walk in and out of the pen rather than climb over it. This all makes me feel like quite a civilized farmer. I fed the geese some bread to go with their cracked corn, as they too rejected the hominy, and gave them clean water for the fifth time today, they seem to dirty it so often, all the while feeling as if some order was finally being attained on this farm. There is something about a barn floor being clean and dry that is very satisfying.

Determined to address directly *something* on the list, I began to unplug the hay chute that had become overloaded this summer when I tried to stop my hay man from throwing any more in my mow. I went to the house and got my favorite and second-best pair of scissors, the ones with shiny brass handles, and went back down to the barn. It was nearly dark. Twilight, in fact, but in the barn it was closer to pitch black. I climbed onto one of the broken beams and peered up the hay chute. The flock surrounded me knowing I was about to put down some hay that they might snack on. I reached above my head, cut the string, and began to pull, all the while hoping I wouldn't drop my scissors into obscurity. It never even occurred to me it could all come down on my head.

The rest of the sheep decided it was time to come in and eat. They have grown quite fat this year, eating hay as well as grass since summer. The corner became crowded. Night fell. And looking up at the loose hay in the chute became a dusty procedure, made especially interesting as I no longer could see a thing. I felt around for the scissors, found where I had dropped them and proceeded up to the house taking an armload of burnable scrap wood with me. The house was fifty-six degrees in both rooms. I made a fire that would improve quickly. I threw some wood in both the stove and fireplace. If only every day were as nice as this one.

THE CARRIAGE HOUSE FARM

WHAT CAN you do since the arrival of the lamb Ally MacBeal? Can you write stories or drink coffee with her sitting nicely on your lap like Mary Queen of Spots or Gilliam MacDouglas's yet-to-be-named little girl? Can you go to the mail-box across the road all alone, enjoying a solitary stroll? Can you walk into your own living room for a civilized moment? Can you visit the new goat and her kids and sit on the bedding and hold one in your lap? Can you go to see if the chickens have resumed laying? No. Of course not.

For this formidable creature of substance, intelligence, personality, and no style has a mind of her own, considers herself an equal and will allow you to do none of the above, at least not without her. With Ally around you do exactly what she and only she wants. Now. This little sheep, for she has never been a lamb, has pushed her head into my hand for me to hold her face. She is too strong for me to keep on my lap, as she can fight her way off in a moment of pushing feet and butting head. She knows how to hit a doorknob to open it, squeeze her head between the doors of the carriage house to jam them open, and when she thinks I am leaving her, she will race down the road after a car that had been parked in my driveway. She doesn't know I don't know how to drive.

As I write, she had tried, over and over, to lift the table with her head and get me to pet her. She will drive me crazy. She is the delight of all visitors who cannot quite imagine how a sheep could be so incredibly bright. Maybe it's chosen to live in the carriage house with the donkey, goats, and chickens. In a few days the cows will be there as well. When she can get in, she loves the house. My fax machine is still kept on the floor and she has managed to chew many pages from it.

I've chosen which of the lambs are to stay. And haven't named them yet. One or two are emotional decisions. There is a lamb that is simply pretty, with the prettiest fleece. She is very relaxed and lets herself be picked up. Some are daughters of mothers whose days are running out. It seems only right that they replace themselves; even the most splendid Ally MacBeal is the daughter of the redoubtable #17, one of the first ewes born here, who is a pure Dorset. Her mother is eight or nine years old. This sturdy, willful little creature is a worthy replacement. It is easy to think so as she has now put her head once more in my hand to have her face and neck petted. She can be nice. She really can. My favorites are more delicate and pretty. She won't ever grow up to be anything but a massive Dorset. No grace, no style. But a lot of brains. Her eyes close. She's still standing, head nestled in my hand. Everyone will love her. But she will never flock or be a sheep. And sometimes I shall feel that she has driven me quite out of my mind. Nonetheless, she shall remain here forever.

There are some combinations of animals that are a simple delight. It is hard to tell exactly why, and yet their enchantment is infectious. Giuseppe Nunzio Patrick MacGuire has spent a great deal of time in the carriage house this month past. Accompanying him is my band of roosters. They are an all-night playing band, indeed. One in particular favors Nunzio and loves to stand on the very edge of his stall, eye level, and crow his heart out to the donkey. He is my favorite rooster, cream, mustard, steel gray, and iridescent green. There was originally a pair of them. My heart broke when I found one dead, murdered, it would seem, by my cat at the time, the original Prentice. Now there is a father-son combination that makes an increasingly splendid pair.

The three barn cats have decided that while field and brook are an endless source of interest, the carriage house is preferable to the barn. They have taken up in there somewhere, I'm not even certain of the exact spot. I had read in a fifteenth-century book that cats are best fed at eleven in the morning. They then take a brief afternoon nap and are relaxed for an evening's hunting expedition. Since none of my bags of grain show any signs of mice or rats having taken their eleven o'clock lunch from them, I suspect my marmalade duo, Prentice and Prescott, along with the gray-and-white Pierce, are doing what they were hired to do.

The carriage house chickens are looking winter weary while their out-of-doors counterparts have a sprightly eagerness to their demeanors that is a pleasure to behold. The roosters tend to cluster around the indoor chickens; however, I suspect it's because there is a lot of grain scattered about the floor. Two of the less beautiful shall be finding their way into my stew pot this weekend. The rest shall stay as long as they live.

The carriage house has become a farm on its own. Ally lives there, having made her own place in which to spend the night and take daytime naps in the hay. Three bottle lambs are doing better there than within the hustle of the barn and have created a nest beneath the stairs in hay that has fallen in between the cracks. Their nest is separated only by a paddock wall from the three kid goats and their mother. The bucks have learned to venture as far as the third step up on the staircase to the chicken coop. They are black and white, and black, and are more adorable than I would wish. They remind me of Colvin who, with his brother, was to have pulled a cart for me long before Nunzio was even a dream. The doe is the prettiest I have ever seen, all chocolate brown with a brilliant and soft coat.

Together Ally MacBeal and Mary Queen of Spots, Anabella Boxer and Lavinia Honeywell, Giuseppe Nunzio Patrick MacGuire, the rooster Zorro and his band, Prentice, Prescott, and Pierce plus the assorted chickens and as yet unnamed goats all have created, in the carriage house, a tiny farm all of its own on my bigger farm. The atmosphere is enchanting. It draws me throughout the day and several times a night. It has its own magic that simply captures the heart. And for that I am grateful in particular to the redoubtable Ally MacBeal.

TWO WOMEN IN THE KITCHEN

T HERE IS a houseguest here at Greenleaf. She has been here for nearly two weeks. She kept house for herself and her family for sixty years. Until she came here. We now, in a manner of speaking, keep house for each other. She is more tolerant of me than I am of her, which is rather an amazing thing to me. She is here for a while because I am supposed to be the understanding one of the two of us. And she needs a lot of understanding. She is renowned for her housekeeping abilities, something for which I am not. "This room is a mess," she shouted at me, staring at my unmade bed the other afternoon. Since the floor and windows were newly washed and each thing in the room had been dusted and polished to within an inch of its life in anticipation of her arrival and fear of her critical eye, I was crushed at the injustice of it. "It's my room," was all I could reply as she kept saying, "Look at that bed, look at that bed. Oh, its your room, then it is okay, honey. We'll just shut the door."

Were I only so absolutely tolerant when I find my dish towels all decoratively placed over the backs of my kitchen chairs, all but covering the newly washed and ironed pillowcases on all of the newly arranged little pillows. I was so proud of getting all of those pillows in order. And so I take the dish towels off and put them away, only to find them draped decoratively across the backs again. I concede. With reluctance, and certainly not with the tolerance that she has shown me in the incident of the unmade bed. I expected but did not receive a hard time about food. My cooking is European, but country and mostly French. My guest's parents were from Italy. Tales of the days when ravioli was made and spread to dry all over the house reached my ears before I ever met her. She and her sisters and mother made them all day. In a time before pasta machines were in every department store.

And so I knew I'd have to try really hard to get the food right. I started with coffee, Maxwell House French Roast. That was an immediate success. Dark, with only a little milk, one sugar. "Mmm, this tastes like chocolate," she said. I breathed a sigh of relief. An omelet was next. Neat. Nothing in it but a pinch of salt and a lot of butter. Light. Very fluffy. Very even. Golden brown. Pale gold. French. Not like the Italian frittatas with a toasty crust. "Wow" came after the first taste. I got an "okay" on a hamburger, something I really don't know how to make. But I haven't struck out. Not yet, at least. Even a desperate version of New England corn chowder passed muster. My potatoes had frozen. I had put them in a box of hay as an insulator, in the dining room. They never made it to the root cellar. When I went into the dining room and uncovered them, they were frozen rocks. All I had to use was corn, rice, bacon, onions, milk, and a lump of butter. Luck has been with me. She loved the chowder.

Making macaroni has been another story altogether. I knew I was on very dangerous waters with that one. She recognized the dough as I made it, beginner's luck, for the first time. And proceeded to tell me why I shouldn't make it. I continued anyway. I made very nice egg dough, oval in shape, put a cloth napkin over it, and set it to rest. All the while she lectured me on the simplicity, the thriftiness, the ease of simply buying a package of macaroni. "You can get enough in one box for three times," she said. Again and again. "For thirty-nine cents." She lifted the napkin and looked again at the dough. "Throw it in the garbage. It's disgusting," she said. I ran it through the pasta machine. "Look, it's going all over the tablecloth. Throw it in the garbage. It's too much work." I sliced the dough and ran it through the machine six times. And then through the slicer again to the dismay of my houseguest.

Later, I made her supper. And made the macaroni for myself. I put her meal in front of her. And silently ate the homemade pasta smothered in butter and Parmesan cheese. I'd glance at her as I ate, my head down, seeing her glance back. "Want some?"

"No."

"Ever make macaroni with your mother?"

"No."

"Want to invite your granddaughter over and we'll make some?"

"She won't come."

I've been reading Italian cookbooks to try to find some things to please her. One described the great pride the women of Bari took in their macaroni-making skills. That was where her mother was from. There were a number of recipes for ravioli. Today I asked her if she ever made ravioli with spinach and ricotta. "Only ricotta," she said. This woman who never had made macaroni of any kind in her life. She had said. She took some spoons from the silverware drawer. "This one, half full, like that, of ricotta only," she said. She who had no knowledge of making macaroni. "Then you eat it with a little Parmesan on the top. On Sundays."

"Right. Shall we make some? I'll buy some ricotta."

"Maybe," she said.

"We'll invite your granddaughter."

"Yes."

"Where does this go?" She asks me. "I want to help. Where does this go?" How do I tell her, this woman in constant motion, pacing up and down my kitchen, that her eighty-year-old eyes are failing and the dishes aren't quite clean enough. "Put them on the table, I'll put them away, thank you," has worked so far, but I won't get away with that much longer. She may know because she has started to polish them dry, rubbing them with a dishcloth.

There are some things at which she is a wonder. Folding laundry is one of them. Slap, slap go the pillowcases in the air. An ancient sound. An absolutely female sound that women have been making when pulling clothes off of clotheslines or placed out to dry in the sun since the beginning of time. Slap. Slap. Then fold. And that one last motion, a pat, as each piece creates a pile.

One of my many Waterloos is the laundry pile. I'm great at washing. Great at drying. Terrible at folding and putting away. Now here is my guest. Most formidable as an attacker, par excellence, on piles of warm and dry miscellaneous tangled clothes. I never knew I had so much stuff. She even has gotten me to put those beautifully folded, nearly organized things away. In their place. Amazing. Absolutely amazing. Who would have believed I'd ever change?

She walks around my kitchen speaking to inanimate objects as if they have a life. "You're in your place," she says with great firmness. "Stay there." How many times I have thought to the very same objects, how did you get here or there or elsewhere? How? Now I have my new friend to say, "Stay in place. Stay in place." God bless you.

Every day she puts on eyebrow pencil and lipstick. Her hair is beautiful, with elegant waves. A startlingly brilliant white. She puts a little bit of Deb on it to keep it pretty. She puts out her clothes at night for the next day. I have a lot to learn. She looks in absolute amazement at my hair when I pull off my barn hat. "You don't care what your hair looks like?" she asks. The funny thing is, I'm often tempted to ask her if I can try a little of her Deb. And when I lend her my lipstick to try the color, I'm tempted to put some on myself as well.

She likes the sound of my name and says it often. "Sylvia, where are you?" When we are both in the same room but I am not in her line of vision.

"Here I am. I'm right here." Two women in the kitchen.

THE UGLY CHICKEN

T HE HEN had been given to me as a throwaway. She and her companion were the ugliest I had ever seen. Not being one to say no to a free animal of any kind, I took them. What their prior owners had neglected to mention was that they didn't lay eggs. One of the two died. Almost immediately. The other, a hideous creature, took off with one of my roosters and became the most free-range of free-range chickens ever to be seen on this farm. She'd manifest in the most unlikely of places, across the road, on a stone wall quite obscured by brush. Or near the white barn next door. Everywhere. Then she started to lay eggs. Blue ones. Immediately I began to admire her and even like her, but she didn't like me. At all. Especially as I began to take the eggs away from her. A good friend is an artist and loves to paint pictures of those tiny blue eggs. And so I had a special use for them.

This year the hen chose an especially nice spot in which to make a nest. It was outside of my chicken coop, of course, but nearby in some hay scraps that had gathered in a corner immediately on its outer edge. I was delighted. Yet there were no eggs to be found. Ever.

A couple of days ago I was in the carriage house loft feeding the geese. There was the ugly little hen. She had nested between the floorboards and wall joists. The space was just the right size to accommodate her small size. I took her off of it for a moment and counted eleven eggs. Blue. I put her back, dumbfounded. Yesterday

I saw her fuddling her way out of the carriage house door surrounded by eight baby chicks. I ran back upstairs to the loft. There were still eight eggs in the nest. And there in the now-vacant winter chicken coop was a chicken I hadn't noticed before sitting in a nesting box. I saw the hole in the netting where she had gained entrance. But why? Who was she? From where had she come? There was no longer anything to eat up there. What could have drawn her? Were the additional eggs hers? And if not, whose?

The chicks were only a few hours old and were quite easy to catch. Their counterparts, the three baby chicks born a couple of weeks ago, had not been, and I've left them to their mother's devices and luck. With two barn cats around the third, Pierce, has taken to hanging around at the neighbor's and assorted other treacheries that abound here, I've not enough trust that this one hen will manage all eight chicks. My fears may be misguided, however, as I watched her try to push one back up a stone stair using her head as a rather unsuccessful lever.

With some help, I managed to get all of the chicks into my trash bin and then, wonder of wonders, the mother hen walked, quite by accident, into a cage nearby. She was immediately incorporated into the tiny flock in the trash bin.

Ernest Westcott and Jim Wilson came down from the side hill having finished the messiest part of the fencing today. Ernest has farmed all of his life. He also has been blessed with the instincts of a farmer. He promptly fashioned the perfect cage for the mother hen and assured me that while the chicks could get in and out of it, she'd call to them and keep them in line. She has. I've put some cracked corn and water and chopped hay in there for them. Last night she had all eight under wing. Today two gray, two black, two brown, and two yellowish chicks are popping in and out of the cage.

The mother hen is amazingly calm in confinement. This, my most outrageous chicken who has never allowed me within ten feet of her, is now sitting calmly as I approach. She acts only mildly perturbed when I drop some fresh food into her cage and is unflustered when the dogs approach. In all, she seems immeasurably altered by her experiences as a mother hen. She is watched inter-mittently by all manner of the wanderers, seems absolutely contented in her cage, all chicks within her sight or under her wing.

The geese have managed to keep one of the two goslings that remain. One disappeared shortly after it was born. The other is beginning to change color. The geese have never moved from the security of the loft of the carriage house where they had made a nest on an old cushion (or rather I had made the nest on the old cushion, having moved their eggs from their nest on the floor). I bring them sod from the vegetable garden to have green grass; a great deal of water served out in dishes of varying sizes to accommodate goose, gander, and gosling, as well as some cracked corn. They guide their charge with their heads and push it to wherever they have decided it is the best advantage. I remain the enemy. Or rather, as I am expected to bring them their food, I am regarded as an enemy to be tolerated. A bucket serves to let them wash their faces and pat water on the gosling. They have abandoned the nest but not the loft and yet in other ways seem to have created a home for themselves. They lack the courage of the mother hens who take their chicks into the world with such immediacy and aplomb.

Two chicks had been hatched by a much beleaguered little chicken the day before shearing. She had been sitting on her refuge behind a wooden pallet leaning against the wall on the upper level of the barn. She never realized that she could most clearly be seen at all times as her head was facing inward into the darkness caused by the shadow of the pallet. Her back bore the scars of many attacks by my outstanding flock of roosters. She is only a year old, born here, and quite inexperienced in the ways of being a hen.

The chicks must have hatched in the morning because it wasn't until afternoon that my son and I came upon them. They were both one flight down from where they were hatched, and could they run! We dove and dashed and ran and chased. Each time I'd think I had my fingers around one, it slipped through them. I'm always afraid I'll hurt a young chick and never quite get my fingers tight enough around it.

One slipped off of the floor's edge down between two walls. I was certain I had driven it to its death. The second hid in all manner of awkward places, eluding capture in every instance. Their mother was beside herself, alternately looking for them and chasing us away. Miraculously, her back feathers had regrown and she suddenly lost her fragile appearance. *She* had become a *hen*. I was heartbroken thinking she'd never find them.

The following morning there she was, clucking and pecking next to her sister, the first hen with chicks this year, and racing in front of her were her two, saved from the corners and cracks in the barn. Chickens count very well to two. And those two hens managed very nicely to keep track of their little ones while making dwelling places they abandon and relocate with great regularity.

The geese have to count only to one to know where their gosling is. But to count to eight is another task altogether. My little ugly hen seems to know, however, when one or two or even three of her chicks are not under her wing and watches them with great intensity. Her get-over-here-now cluck is easily interpreted by them, and they are well-behaved little chicks, racing back into her cage when she demands their obedience. I check on them with great frequency. That means all day long. It is a delight. With any luck they will not be as skittish as their mother hen. With a bit more luck than that they might all make it.

MIRACLES GREAT AND SMALL

THE BARNYARD has been cleared of debris. The remnants from the collapse of the south wall of the barn two years ago are all gone. Or rather, the broken beams are neatly stacked, and forty huge piles of manure have been distributed in perfect order around the pastures. It is not, in fact, gone at all, none of it, but instead repositioned to more useful places. The grass near the piles has already turned a dark green. Dew trapped in the manure has quickened the slow release of its fertilizer and given small droplets of water to the drought-stricken pasture. I am grateful beyond imagination and haven't a clue about how to express it.

Yesterday I was given a hundred tomato plants for a mere ten dollars. And some fertilizer and advice thrown in. The advice was invaluable. One flat was of yellow tomatoes, which make the best jam in the world with all due respect to red tomatoes. The other flat, somewhat in distress, was of Roma tomatoes. If they make it, they will replace ones I bought from Georgia that are failing.

I have been working relentlessly on the vegetable garden and have high hopes for it. Some of it is planted, but much is waiting for me first to move the chickens to an enclosure that will prevent them from nibbling on the seeds. The ground where I planted some bean seeds had been well fluffed up by my rooster collection the day after the planting. I have only a few more days to see if it needs be replanted. Should anything have sprouted, all will be declared well.

One morning I was in the garden far before dawn. Worries of a practical nature had plagued me all night and it made no sense to stay indoors any longer. Light had come from the east before the sun. A neighbor down the valley was playing music. It floated on the morning mist. It was very beautiful. I dug in the garden all morning and for most of the day with renewed joy and strength. I have since added to the stone paths and am now an hour or two away from completing the redigging of the original garden. All that shall be left by this time tomorrow is the section that shall hold its expansion. And that, too, is partially done.

It feels as if I am smashing down relentlessly all of the obstacles that are preventing this farm from succeeding, one at a time. The lessons learned from the fence have made a deep impression on me. But there are other lessons as well, some of which I've had inklings of for my whole life but had never become part of me. Some of the debris from the barn is the result of tasks that I have only partially completed. There is an old semidemolished feeder in which I have gathered plastics, both of which I have been intending to throw away. And there they have sat for a very long time. I now think it is best to do all of something and to seem to accomplish less, than to do part of many things. Nothing here has ever been totally neglected, because I have been evenhanded in performing my allotted tasks. But nothing is totally completed, either. I have decided to complete each task one day at a time in its entirety before going on to the next. It is summer, today, so nothing will seriously suffer if I try this experiment. I remember the desperate day one winter I started to shovel the cow manure from the stall out of the barn window. I resolved then to immediately spread it onto the fields. It sits there still, much shrunk, but in its original pile, soon to be moved by machine onto the field. The cow manure shall never again be piled anywhere except, at worst, into a wheelbarrow outside of the window unless it is to be immediately spread.

In its own way, the manure now being dumped onto the fields is an extraordinary gift. The parched earth is desperate. The nutrients and the abundance of good things being bestowed upon it must be received with equal gratitude. The sheep will not graze next to spread manure no matter how decomposed it is, and so the newly flushed grass shall be spared. With any luck, it shall be spared until fall.

The blessings that have been bestowed upon us this year have been received with a heart full of gratitude. However, there is an element of distrust that, with an insidious consistency, tries to use up the presence of joy in the human heart. It whispers, "Do not speak of the good that has befallen you because it shall then be taken from you. Do not say a child is beautiful for the wicked fairy will then take it away." But there are no jealous gods waiting to snatch good from our lives. Only jealous people. And even they may be simply impoverished souls who fear to allow love to enter their hearts. Nonetheless, we still fear sometimes to tell each other our blessings, hearing ancient warnings in the back of our thoughts, warnings that they shall be taken from us. But then how do we sing out thanks? And celebrate gratitude?

There has been a grand assortment of blessings here of late. Some have been in the form of a box of white shirts, enough to wear a different one every day for more than two weeks. And yellow tomatoes at half price. And a dear friend to run around town with sometimes and bring me Epsom salts. And a kind and generous person who is shoveling the barn for us, for the sheep and me, that is. And a gracious friend who has told her waiters that I am a guest of the house when I snatch a rare moment to have lunch at her restaurant. And the friend who brought me enough crystal green first-cut hay to feed my most prolific sheep next winter, besides going out of his way to bring me store cheese whenever he comes to work for me.

My front apartment tenants are a joy to share the house with. And even the elderly lady who is staying with me for a while is a blessing, because the only good she can still remember in life is love. The sheep have grown fat for some amazing and no understood reason on the parched earth. And dear friends are taking some of them for the summer to relieve the stresses on the pasture.

There are even more blessings to be counted. And I shall.

SUMMER ON THE FARM

THERE IS a chicken that I have forgotten. A brown hen with spurs on her feet. It is not distinguished by anything exceptional, markings or color, or personality, for that matter. A chicken most easy to forget.

I found her today in the cow manger surrounded by a dozen little chickens. Tiny little chickens. Six black or steel gray, reminders of Zorro the fighter rooster who lived here for a little too long, and six yellow with a brown or, rather, sienna stripe. Very pretty little chickens.

I don't quite know what to do. The outdoor nesting box has the fiercest fighting chicken on the farm in it, the famous layer of blue eggs. She has spurs bigger than her beak, attacks at no provocation whatsoever, and clucks furiously when any of her surviving six baby chicks are out of sight. She is content, if that word could ever be used to describe this chicken, only if all of her chicks are either under or over her wing. (They are too big to all fit under her tiny wings any longer and some now simply sit on her back.) Those are the only times I've ever seen her sitting still. She occupies the baby chick–mother hen cage of choice by my back porch steps. There is only one. What to do? I don't want to let her go free. She is the kind of chicken who inevitably finds her way into the garden. If only one chicken feels like pecking someone else's chicks, she is the one.

What to do with the russet hen and her chicks? Furthermore, where are my little henna hen and the partridge-feathered one who raised a little flock this spring? I think I'm short two more chickens. Could they be brooding? And shall I be feeding a massive number of chickens all winter, waiting to see which sprout tail feathers indicating that they are roosters and subsequently needing someone to butcher them for me?

One of the clutch of four born a couple of months ago may be a black rooster. He is smaller and has longer tail feathers than the three with whom he was hatched out. I have no way to tell what any of the six of the blue-egg hen might be. Nor the twelve in the manger. Nor the three racing after the orange hen in the barnyard. Of course I prefer hens to roosters. I have too many roosters.

I count, recount, and recount again, each time devising a new system with which to categorize the chickens. Each time I come up with a new number. At the moment I think I have three pullets, five chickens, four big chicks, six little ones, three other little ones, twelve newly hatched chicks, twenty-five Barred Plymouth Rocks, and eleven, more or less, roosters. I think that's it. But I'm not quite sure.

The blueberries are magnificent this year. There are bushes so heavily laden as to seem more black than green. I've gone up the hill to pick them several times this past week. Gradually they jumped the wide band of woods that surrounds the upper flat where they were first found and established themselves on the slope of the hill. The slope is now covered with tiny bushes low to the ground as well as a tall one, five feet tall or so, literally covered with ripe berries. Naturally, there is a human tradition in gathering berries. That tradition is one for the mouth, one for the berry basket. What was learned that was most revealing from this practice was that each bush had different-tasting berries. Some were sweet. Some were tart. Some barely had a taste, and only one or two tasted classically, perfectly of blueberry. A friend came with me up the hill today. She had never picked blueberries before. She made the same observation.

What she couldn't have known, having nothing with which to make a comparison, was how thickly the bushes were laden. Thoughts of bears began to slip in between thought of the blueberries. I have hesitated to go alone berrying on the top of my hill for quite some time. I still go, despite some minor apprehension. But I am more cautious than I have been and go only on the spur of the moment, on impulse; never can I walk that steep hill with intent to go into the blueberry fields.

Chokecherries are not as plentiful this year as they have been. They make the most beautiful syrup I have ever seen, a cross between magenta and red. I've started saving bottles in which to store it. The blackberries are growing thickly as well. I've been looking at recipes in French cookbooks to learn to make wine from them as well as jam. I left a stand of bushes beside the new wooden fence, in part because the flowers were so lovely. Now I rejoice at the sight of them, thick and heavily laden, and think of evenings walking outside with a bowl of cream in one hand and a spoon in the other, picking thick sweet berries to have for dinner under a tree.

This is the sweet time of the year. Summer lambs are being born, as well as baby chicks. There are two and their dam in the lambing room today. A ram and a ewe. Their mother freshened in January as well. She was a carefully considered decision. Eight years old, a beautiful confirmation, a Dorset-Finn cross, and a perfect mother, who could not nurse her lamb. I kept her, never dreaming she'd drop twins six months later. In all actuality, she is turning a greater profit, even if I have to buy milk replacer, than a ewe who had only a single. I only hope she freshens in the spring rather than the winter next time. I can't handle winter bottle lambs.

This is the sweet time on the farm as well. Walking up the hill for berries or to look at the progress of the fence. Finding baby chicks and their mother hen. Watching the Barred Rocks grow up. Seeing patches of green around the newly spread barnyard manure. And holding baby lambs, training them to come to me. The paths made when the fields were brush hogged have added a gracefulness to the sweep of meadow that was never perceived before. Summer on the farm.

TO PATRICIA, FROM EAST LYME

I T W O U L D appear that men and women have different approaches to the way one must run a farm. I have no data to which
I might compare this observation, only eleven and a half years of
experience running my farm. Alone. And so I admit immediately
before saying another word that there is a strong possibility that I
could be wrong, and I readily admit that my observations are purely
subjective. Nonetheless, I've been the recipient of a number of
suggestions recently that have led me to think I might be correct.

Take the placement of my new corn feeder as an example. I had
dragged the twelve-foot-long platform from the front of the house,
across the backyard, through the gate, and down the slope, laying it
to rest temporarily on a discarded beam somewhat near the barn. I
wanted legs to be put on it to raise it off of the ground. My
preference was to have it placed on two legs with a carriage bolt on
each end so it could be turned over and cleaned if needed. Each leg
would have a long foot on the end to make it tipproof. It seemed to
me, however, that the feeder was too long to be stable if built that
way unless I were to have two legs on swivels on the sides that could
hold the manger rigid when it was not being turned. Nonetheless,
after I had the legs installed, I wanted the manger moved relatively
close to the little low door that I had to pass through every day
carrying the grain. I didn't want to walk down an icy slope in the
winter with fifty pounds of grain divided between two buckets in my
hands. Their combined weight would lower my center of gravity

and, as I moved both forward and down, would encourage a fall. The man building the feeder saw things otherwise. I had simply told him where I wanted the feeder positioned when he was finished and went on my way. A big mistake. Upon my return I found the legs neatly installed and the feeder firmly ensconced about thirty feet away from the place most convenient for my use. "Oh, it will get rain on it from the roof were I to put it where you wanted it," I was told. "I didn't want it to get ruined," said he. I said nothing.

My mother was raised by a Victorian mother and therefore was firmly convinced of an inherent weakness in all men (that is, all men, not all of mankind). Men are fragile creatures whose feelings get hurt easily and must be spared as much as possible from "things." "Things" meant all manner of situations, problems, or affronts to the ego. "*They* are not as strong as women," my mother would say. "*They* can't take what we can. They fall apart easily. You have to be careful about how you say things to *them*." And so these words and a variation thereof have been engraved on my soul. Therefore, I was reluctant to say to my hired man what I thought, which was, in no uncertain terms, that it is scientifically impossible for any more rain to fall into this feeder in the spot where it is most useful to me than in the spot from which he did not wish to move it.

I let my annoyance with the arrangement build up for a couple of days in order for it to give me the strength to dislodge the feeder, now well frozen into the ground. It took several wallops with the head of an axe accompanied by a fury that had for its inspiration my repeatedly tripping over the indentations of frozen mud to move it to a position convenient to me. I shall say nothing to its builder when I have already paid for the privilege of the experience.

Then there was the suggestion from someone who claims to have had experience on a sheep farm on how best to feed out my hay. I shall not go into the arduousness of the logistics I go through each day to accomplish that. Just saying that it is almost the most inefficient method conceivable should be enough. Last year's system was the most inefficient conceivable. This year's goes beyond that. I'm making progress on my quest to learn patience and the value of the advice "all things in God's time, not my time." It was suggested in all seriousness that I move the sheep outside, drop hay on the dirty floor, and fork it into mangers that are situated between fifteen and thirty-two feet away from the hay chute.

I am paying a king's ransom for hay this winter. A mouthful soiled is a mouthful wasted. The winter door in the barn is only two and a half feet wide. The sheep are pregnant. The north barn door, the only one I have, has solid ice in the ditches in front of it made by the skid steerer that was used to clean out the barn. Its operator was to return to level things off before the ice became solid; however, he didn't. It is the exact texture and thickness to break when stepped on, cut a sheep's ankle, and trap it in ice water. It is not difficult to see why the sheep are reluctant to leave the building upon facing the ice through that door or why they often turn around to reenter the barn while their friends and relatives are still trying to get out. How long would this little exercise take, one might ask oneself, two or three times a day at that. An hour each time?

Sheep have been maligned for a very long time, considered to be not the brightest of God's creatures. Poor dear things. Because they are docile when they know they are loved by a good shepherd, they have been profoundly misunderstood by mankind.

My sheep know certain things. It is a limited number of things, but know them they do. They know when I am in a bad mood and they need behave. They know when I am going to fix a wound or pull a lamb that has become tangled within them and let me do it. They know to stand in a group when I am fussing over them in the evening in the barn, when chores are finished and we can simply be together, and they butt in only if I've spent too much time with the one ahead of them. They know if I am trying to trick them and let me get away with it only once, to humor me. Were I to put the sheep, all hundred plus whatever lambs there might be, outside and proceed to fill the mangers inside with food, would they ever let me repeat the exercise again? No . . . well, maybe some of them, those who wanted a drink at the brook or a romp more than they wanted hay. The rest would simply stay inside and stomp on the hay as I dropped it down the chute. And I'd have to fight them off with a pitchfork in my hand. Now would anyone capable of logical thought think this is a sane activity for sheep or shepherd? When I looked incredulous at the suggestion, the person making it said, "Well, maybe you just can't understand what I am saying."

Then there was the contractor who couldn't understand why I wouldn't line my barn with aluminum-faced fiberboard insulation and told me just to open the door to the barn if the ammonia buildup from a hundred sheep became too much for me to breathe. Not to mention the hay dealer who swore to me that a dusty white powder always flies out of late-cut hay. "The sheep will eat it if that's all they've got." Similar in fact to deer that are found dead from starvation with bellies full of pine needles, or people, in times of war, who have eaten paper out of sheer desperation.

The issue, if there were one, would seem to be about values. Is the object a feeder, a bale of hay, a sale, the thing to be most valued, or is the living thing, the stock, the laborer more important? My mother would tell me, were she alive, to tear up this story. God bless her.

THE COLOR WHITE

T HE STUFF that dreams are made of comes in all manner of shapes, forms, textures, and colors. For me, sometimes it is the noncolor white that inspires and encourages, and today it is the white of sheets of paper, foolscap with a magenta double line down its side and pale blue stripes on which to write. It is the white of pages in new paperback books and the newly starched white of my kitchen curtains and tablecloth as well as the white of this typewritten page.

I applied today for a grant to obtain money to learn how to train my donkey, Giuseppe Nunzio Patrick MacGuire, to work on this farm with me. When he was first here, I was assured that he knew how to draw a cart, and when put through his paces by an expert in donkeydom, I was assured again that, indeed, Nunzio knew how to work. It is I who doesn't. I've never been an animal person in that way, the way that is based on a natural ease, an inborn affinity and understanding. On the other hand, once an animal becomes mine, suddenly something happens. It is beyond me what that something is, but something does, and then all is in accord much of the time.

Training is, however, something else. I recognize that. I know nothing about it and so my request for a grant. I included the need for lessons on how to drive Nunzio. I also included the making of a harness for him. At a horse auction one day, I accosted an Amish man who was selling all manner of tack. He was a harness maker. I told him he would hear from me, not immediately, but would hear from me nonetheless. He is my choice to make the harness for Nunzio.

In a way, simply writing the grant proposal brought me even closer to the dream of working this farm the way it requests me to. Putting the dream on paper, blue ink on white paper, gave it clarity that it had not possessed before, a definition, and integration between itself and other parts of this life here on my farm. As if the act of stating a wish could, in itself, create the desired effect.

I remember the day I first decided I wanted a donkey. I had been raised by my farm girl mother who had hitched a team of horses each morning to drive them to the one-room schoolhouse where she taught farm children grades kindergarten through eighth, ages five through eighteen. In those days, in East Lyme, Connecticut, farm boys most often went to school after harvest and only until planting in early March. And so eight years of grammar school often stretched over twelve. My mother told me stories about taking the horses to school through the snow in winters. And the morning an enormous snake hung down from the branch of a tree in front of the team as she was racing, late to school. The horses bolted with my mother at the reins. The image has remained with me over all of these years. And I absorbed the fear, not my mother's but the fear experienced by the horses. She accompanied the story with the one about her cousin, paralyzed from the waist down after a fall from another spooked horse. In all fairness she also told me about my beloved aunt Til who loved to ride one of the horses bareback, her chestnut hair blowing in the wind, in the pasture of my grandfather's farm. I know that a horse is not a donkey, but I also know I was raised to be afraid of all form of equines, and a donkey is not much different. It is an equine.

One April day the second or third spring after starting this farm, I received a package in the mail. I had sold a lamb and taken a salary for the very first time. With it I bought a book about farming. I took the package and went out into the south pasture. I sat on a stone wall under a vast cherry tree just beginning to be edged in pale green, and

I opened the package. The book was to become one of the most influential forces guiding this farm. First issued at the close of the last century, it described hundred-year-old farm methods and how to execute them. Included was a drawing of a four-sided drag made very much like the wooden rack in which people used to keep tennis rackets. In between the frames were pinned branches from thorn apple trees. These harrowed the newly plowed fields. I was enchanted. I wanted to make one of these frames, and I wanted to use it on my farm. Not that I plowed. But to create a surface on which to frost-sow clover and even, with some modifications, to clear the driveway of snow. But to use it required a horse. No. A donkey. Yes.

The book was published by Alan Hood in Brattleboro, Vermont. I called him and sometime later got a second book. A similar inspiration. Since then Lyons Press in New York has begun to publish reprints of other old farm books, and one way or another I have most of them.

This year I promised myself to do no further reconstruction of the barn. There is no money for anything remotely to be considered extra down there. Buying enough hay and grain will be hard enough. There is not enough money for lumber. Today, however, I am unable to restrain myself from dreaming. And so I pulled down the books from my library shelves and against my better judgment am beginning to dream again. It won't cost too much, take very much time, need very much material to build that chicken feeder, hang that old medicine chest in the lambing room, build that four-sided sheep trough. Perhaps I can have some of the bits and pieces that will allow my dream to become reality after all.

The books make a neat stack. The ones from Alan Hood are somewhat larger than those from Lyons Press, but they make a tantalizing grouping. And I am drawn to them. They lie on my kitchen table, on a newly ironed cloth, white and gleaming. The cloth matches the heavily starched freshly hung curtains on the windows on either side of the brand-new kitchen stove that my family just bought me. I knew I'd never accept the gift of the stove until I had solved the problems it presented to my mind. The problems of its newness and its contrast with the old one I clung to for so long. But there is a freshness to it and a promise of creating even more of the life that I so long for. It inspired me to hang the curtains, which in turn inspired me to think. Which in turn reminded me of the grant application that may have been somewhere in my special-things-to-do basket in the living room. Maybe. I hoped. And it was.

MY HIRED MAN

THE CHEVY pickup is the color of cream. The cream of milk from a Jersey cow near the end of her lactation. Its fenders are trimmed in burnt sienna lace, otherwise referred to as rust. I do not refer to it as rust. Its owner is a farmer, heart, soul, and inclination. He is also my hired man. One or two half days a week. He has been seventy-five for three years now. We drive in it. Wednesdays, country music blaring from the radio, Reba McEntire. He loves her hair. He whistles. I listen. Or try to, over the rattle of the engine, the sounds of the road, and the static on the radio.

Wednesday is the only day of the week that I can reliably identify by name. It is the day we go to town. He's tried to change Wednesday to Thursday. He bowls on Wednesday. Plays cards on Tuesday. Needs to be home by four o'clock to feed his cows. I don't know what he does on Sunday or Monday nights. I need Wednesday to be Wednesday. Thursday is too late in the week. Tuesday is too soon. The livestock auction in Unadilla is Wednesday. Every Wednesday enhances the urgency of my choice of the preferable day to go to town.

I've only just begun to go to the auction. It is a dangerous place for me. I've been known to buy a goat to save it from slaughter. I find it too much to be borne to go every week. I have been known on rare occasion to sell some rams at that auction. Against my principles. Seeing my livestock go the truckers to be sold for meat is an experience boarding on Purgatory if not hell for me. The choices, this fall, however, have been reduced to none.

On auction day, Ernest comes early, driving the truck into the barnyard, with ease born of experience, into the loading pen he built and rebuilt (as it fell apart with regularity) for me. It is now in a condition of being rebuilt for what may be the last time. I hope. The rams were all in the lambing room, to separate them from the flock now being bred by my new East Friesian ram. He is a spectacular fellow. Big. Showy. Tame. He is the future of the farm. My farm. The East Friesian breed is the milk breed of the world of sheep. Holstein-Friesians are the mammoth milk producers of the world of cows. East Friesian sheep originally came from the same neck of the woods. They are heavy milk producers. The ewes of the breed, of course. However, the Finn-Landrace breed of sheep produce milk heavier in the essential milk solids than any others. Dorsets are evaluated somewhere in the middle. The ideal sheep with which to create a sheep milk dairy are an East Friesian lamb and a dam who is a Dorset-Finn cross. I own about ninety Dorset-Finn cross ewes. And am partners in the ownership of one East-Friesian cross ram. By spring many of the ewes will have freshened with the extraordinary crossbred lambs and my dairy flock will officially be on the ground. The hard part is not winter lambing, snow and ice on the stone steps to the barn, temperatures in the low teens and subzero with the windchill factor. The hard part is that I have to sell my other rams so they shall not breed my ewes again. From now on it is only the East Friesian ram, William, Greenleaf Sire, who has that privilege.

I had nine or ten rams in the lambing room. All but two would have to be sold. Prices at the auction vary greatly. Sometimes there are too many sheep and the price is low. Sometimes there are not enough and the prices are even lower. Sometimes there is a Muslim holiday and the price is high. And sometimes it is a Christian one and the price is high or low, depending on the number of buyers on hand

and how saturated the market is. Necessity decreed that I sell three or four at a time, every other week. Russian roulette with prices.

Ernest has been seventy-five for three years now. I've already said that. He has white hair that he cuts when it starts to curl. He is two inches shorter than I am. His hip has been replaced twice and he walks with a slight limp. The second time it was replaced he used a cane for a while. Got into an argument with it one day and threw it away. To load some reluctant rams on to a pickup truck from a small building without a ramp requires careful planning. It requires moving the spare tire from the back of the truck to the top of the cab and tying it on. Then one must string a rope across the truck tight enough to stretch when the rams are tied onto it. We then have to catch the rams. I then have to catch the rams. He can't. We both know it. But pretend we don't. He stands to the side, against the wall, so he won't get trampled as the sheep circle the room. They race, frantically, knowing why we are there. They crowd into a corner. I tied a baling twine rope around the neck of the rams I want to sell. I dragged them, one at a time, to the doorway. Ernest said, "You don't know how to do it. The knot needs to be under the chin." I couldn't turn the rope around and still keep control of the butting, kicking animal. We pulled the rams, one by one, out through the lambing-room door and lifted the thrashing and struggling animals onto the truck. Ernest climbed around the side of the truck squeezing in between it and the gatepost and tied each ram, one at a time, onto the rope.

It is not the same maneuver to drive out of the barnyard as it is to drive into it. There is a pile of wood in the middle of it that successfully manages to disrupt navigation from some angles but not others. Ernest got stuck between the pile of wood and the barnyard fence. He rocked the truck back and forth, his face expressionless, and never said a word. Fifteen minutes later he was out. I climbed into the truck. "You never do your seat belt until you're on the road," I say. Always.

Ernest turns on the radio the moment he starts the engine. We drive country roads. The pretty ones. I hate the highway. And told him once. That I wanted to drive home, country roads. He asked how much longer was the pretty road back to my farm, "the other road." A mile. (I lied. It is two.) Since then he heads to "the other road" on days that he isn't going to bowl or play cards that night.

The foothills of the Catskill Mountains are lovely. This is my life. Riding these hills in this lace-ridden Chevy truck. Fast. Ernest never takes his eyes from the road, driving and listening to Reba McEntire, taking me to the feed store to buy grain, the farm supply store to buy hinges, the Salvation Army to buy Eddie Bauer shirts, and Elena's Pastry Shop to drink espresso and eat cake.

I send Ernest to the feed store while I go to the Salvation Army and Elena's. He says he'll pick me up in an hour. It never is an hour. It is always just enough less for me to not be able to finish my lunch. Or longer enough for me to think he has forgotten me. One day he was an hour and a half late. He said he had forgotten me and drove all the way home when he suddenly remembered I was to be picked up. I believed him. We drove ten miles before he told me he'd been visiting his friend and lost track of time. I was certain he had suddenly begun to lose his mind and was so grateful to realize he hadn't that I wasn't even angry. Ernest charges me fifteen dollars each time he comes. Sometimes he'll raise it to twenty dollars. For six hours of work. I'll add a few dollars to it for gas. Sometimes I don't have any money with which to pay him. I used to say please put the day's work on my tab. I don't anymore. We both seem to understand which days I don't have any money to pay him. On those days he just pulls out of the driveway especially fast when he's finished with work.

Ernest, who has lived here all of his life and been on each road not hundreds but thousands of times, belongs here. He has always belonged. He is familiar. Deeply familiar. I know the roads running through these hills as well and love to look at them, each week changing, sometimes subtly, sometimes with great drama. They are mine, too. But barely. And I feel surrounded, completely surrounded by a world so familiar to him, one in which he, too, is familiar. And am so very much the stranger in it.

THE AWFUL DAY

T HIS HAS been a terrible day. Absolutely awful. It wasn't supposed to be. It didn't even seem to be at first. Even in between the worst it still seemed as if it was going to be a good day.

The kitchen was an absolute mess this morning. I've been mixing a lot of milk replacer. The first bag of the year was full of lumps, some the size of goose eggs, and impossible to mix into a drink that would pass through the nipple on a baby bottle. Somehow I've never devised a foolproof procedure that I can adopt to mix it more easily. It would seem that after all of these years I would have figured out how to do it. But each time I come up with a system I scrap it.

This, the first bag, lent itself to the creation of a series of messes that needed my attention. I've not had hot water for nearly a week, so cleanup was made that much more difficult. When I couldn't get the lumps of dried milk replacer off of my hands, I reached for the phone and explained in no uncertain terms to the manufacturer what I thought of his product. Desperate situations inspire desperate measures. And so I decided that after the most rudimentary of care to my various and sundry charges, I'd clean the kitchen. So I'd be able to come in to a halfway-civilized room each time I returned from the barn. And so I started to heat some water on the kitchen stove. As soon as it was warm enough I ran out with some of that water to the chickens. Life for them has been rough during this cold snap. I usually give them hot mash in the evening but decided to give them some this morning as well. The chicken house in the carriage house is home to a variety of chickens and one rooster. However, the other chickens who were born here and roosters who were, some of them, born here, and some from my friends the Daltons and therefore not born here, have been hovering around the coop picking up whatever they can glean. Spilled corn. Hayseeds, and scraps of laying mash.

There in front of the coop were two roosters. One, pitch black. The other, pure white. Both dead. They had killed each other. They were among the roosters who have been born here. Not my favorites. But they had been earmarked for the pot. I've been wanting to make a chicken in red wine for quite some time and had chosen those two for the pot. The double murders should have told me something. In the coop was another frozen chicken.

A day or two ago I had improperly fastened the barn door. Several sheep had gotten out. Annabel, one of the first ewes born here, freshened. Outside. In the sun. I had been in a rush to get to the barn, and, without looking, threw some hay over the bridgeway wall and raced down the stairs to the mow to begin to toss the requisite fifteen bales of hay. When I went to serve them out, I realized the barn was a little empty. I rushed to the south side and spotted two very fat little lambs in a snowdrift. One was warm enough to have melted the snow, the wet of which proceeded to freeze over its little face. I bundled them up in my scarf and ran to the house. The smaller of the two picked up first, took a bottle and, after an hour surrounded by plastic bottles filled with hot water and well wrapped in towels, jumped out of her basket and began to run around the kitchen. The larger was a little slower. Didn't want a bottle but regained itself nicely anyway. I chose to take her back to the barn and try to locate her mom. I found her. The little lamb dove in and nursed with vigor. The other was disinterested. I couldn't get her to nurse. And so Snow White Abernathy joined the house lambs inside while Rose

Red Abernathy joined her mother. This morning I noticed a little bundle huddled against the hollowed-out pack of the barn going down from the fiasco three years ago. It was Rose Red. Nearly strangled by a piece of baling twine embedded in the pack still there from the day the barn wall collapsed. Cold once more. Limp. Back to the house. She survived, but I could take no more chances. Two chances are a lot on a farm. She has joined her sister in the house.

I managed to get the dishes washed, working out a system of heating water on the stove and soaking the pots in the sink. It felt so good to have the sink empty. I scrubbed down the new stove and part of the rest of the kitchen. Hope slipped in and out of the day. And I began to feel that life could be manageable.

But the barn chores called and I became more and more conflicted. I put the sheep out for water and put hay in the barnyard. Something white peeped out from under a bale I had thrown over. Rooster number three. How in the world I ever could have tossed a bale more than thirty feet above the rooster and managed to hit it on its head and kill it was beyond me. But I did.

Each incident didn't manage to alter the feeling that had pervaded the day from its onset. The day began accompanied by the feeling that life was possible and even, on some level, quite manageable. In between all of the bottling of lambs, feeding out hay, caring for the chickens, geese, and the elderly lady who lives with me, I worked as intensely as I could on putting the house in order so I could live in it more easily. Food has been a distinct problem. I've not had time to cook very much, and while my guest eats some very nice little dishes, I don't. After realizing that I've been eating while walking, standing, and even while climbing the stairs it became apparent I had to cook. And so I managed to make a loaf of bread, a sweet ricotta tart, a spinach pie, and minestrone soup. In between. In between. In between. And it was while in between I heard the old familiar sound of water running. Inappropriately. A pipe had burst on the third floor. And was flooding the apartment next door. With hot water. The tenant's bathroom ceiling had collapsed. I ran over there. Turned off the water. Mopped up the mess. They were not home. And the day didn't get any better.

THE PEARL NECKLACE

O NE O F the yearling lambs, Scout Miller, freshened yesterday. She presented in front of me. I touched the little hooves that had begun to show, making room for a nose and then head. She resented the intrusion. Got up. Walked away. And promptly dropped the lamb. While walking. She seemed shocked. Looked behind her and saw the little bundle. It seemed absolutely bewildered.

I cleaned the mouth of the tiny ewe lamb. She couldn't have weighed two pounds. Only one more lambing pen was ready for occupancy. I put the new mother and her baby in its safe warmth. She licked her baby clean. I decided to leave her alone for a few minutes to bond with her baby and started up the ladder to the house. Suddenly the person building still another lambing jug for the barn called me back. She'd dropped another. The second lamb was even smaller than the first. Pure white. The length of my hand. I helped dry them off and left. Every couple of hours I went back to check on them. I tube-fed each one with a mixture of egg, corn syrup, cod liver oil, and lamb milk replacer, just in case they hadn't enough colostrum, and took their temperatures each time I went to the barn. They were always close enough to a normal temperature to make me begin to feel secure. Those two were lambs to keep. Twin girls out of a twelve-month-old ewe, a lamb herself.

I have a baby monitor in the barn. There is a receiver in the kitchen as well as upstairs. It saves lives. I can rush to the barn whenever I hear the sound of trouble. The two little ewe lambs were noisy, excited, and active.

Six more lambs were born throughout the afternoon and evening. A little ram was born to a most attentive mother. His legs were long and rangy. His voice was nothing short of a bellow as he followed close by his mother's side. She rarely took a step away from him. I saw him nurse and was satisfied with his appearance, even though he looked a bit on the skinny side.

The morning was greeted with a sense of excitement. I rushed to the barn earlier than usual and dashed through a new gate to the lambing pens. The tiniest ewe lamb was running around the jug. The larger was squashed to death between her dam and the wall. In the next pen was the day-old ram, limp but still moving his head. His mother hovered over him. I picked him up, tucked him inside my coveralls, and climbed back up the ladder. I have a fine book on lambing procedures that I got in England one summer. It describes how to discern between hypothermia in lambs due to cold or starvation. Starvation was apparent. Either his mother didn't have her milk come in or he couldn't suck.

I have given intraperitoneal injections of glucose to starving lambs before with only a fifty percent survival rate. One beautiful little lamb called Little Horse, because of her size, lived for six months only to be hit by a car while crossing the road to look for me at the mailbox. The others who didn't make it died after a couple of days. I boiled my needles. Then I mixed a syringe half full with glucose and topped it off with the boiled water to correct the temperature. There is nothing worse for me than giving an injection directly into a lamb's belly. I did it anyway. My syringe was too small to do it all in one or two doses and so I gave him three. Wrapped him in towels with warm bottles next to him, put him in a basket next to the wood stove, and went back down to the barn.

I am introducing the bottle lambs that have lived in a pen in the house back into the barn. The oldest and biggest was practically walking and talking. His leaps in the air after having his bottles were wondrous to behold. He, of all of the lambs, was ready for the move. The first day or two was an adventure. I took him to the walk-through gate over and over again to teach him how to go from the barn proper into the aisle where the lambs join together on the lamb bar and eat grain and second-cutting hay. He needed to be shown a few times before he could find the place on his own.

I checked the remaining of Scout Miller's twins. She is a quarter Finn-Landrace but looks like a classic little Finn. Talks like one, too. Aggressive, bright, alert, and less than two pounds. She was warm and toasty in the jug with her dam. Her fleece had dried out and emerged both thick and curly. A classic Finn although her sire is a pure Dorset (well, a Dorset with a sixteenth Cheviot in him). Thank goodness she was safe. And then I saw him. Red ribbon around his neck. Right next to the gate that I had taught him to walk through. Dead. He had been squashed to death by some grown sheep. The temperature in the barn dropped twenty degrees, in minutes. In an hour I started putting sweaters back on. I went back to the house, started the fires, tube-fed the weak lamb. He took two ounces on his own and let himself be tucked back in his basket. The temperature continued to drop. Evening approached. It was time to go to the barn again. Everyone had been fed. All chores were done. But I like to go down twice again during the night. I went from the warm kitchen into the unheated living room to get my coveralls. And became, suddenly, chilled to the marrow of my bones. I couldn't go out again that night. Sometimes the heart can handle only so much. And then it becomes just too cold.

Scout Miller's lamb is enchanting. This morning I heard her voice, a valiant little tin horn sound, absolutely frantic. Somehow she had slipped between the cracks of the lambing jugs and was separated from her mother by two-inch-thick boards. She was desperately trying to get to her dam. I ran over to the jug. Before I got to her she had squeezed her head and front legs into the gap I use to climb over the walls and was scrambling to get her back legs back in. I let her try it on her own. She made it. Finns are very intelligent. I was so proud of her, and so pleased with Scout. I handle the ewe lamb as often as I can. Her tummy is always full. Her little Finn tail is always wagging. And she has presence, as rare a quality in a sheep as it is in a person. I've penned a ewe who hates her lamb in my new stanchions. Her baby ram is absolutely beautiful. He has a curly fleece as well, and one droopy ear. And a mother who hates him. After a week in the stanchion she still doesn't want him to nurse. I release her from time to time to see if she will appreciate him better when her head is not locked. But she still tries to destroy him when he comes near her. So back into the stanchion she goes. The stanchion walls are now lined in tarpaper to keep the lamb and his mom that much more comfortable. One of my favorite ewes, Jenny, has just given birth to a fine set of lambs, twin ewes. I had sold Jenny to a friend who was buying breeding stock a couple of years ago. When he decided sheep were too demanding, he gave her back to me as a gift. Each year she has an adorable set of twin ewe lambs. They, too, are Finn crosses. Jenny is half Finn. Their dad is a pure Dorset. They are bright little things, far more alert and personable than other lambs only two or three days old. They always draw my eye. I decided they too should move into the stanchion with their mom. Jenny doesn't need to be penned, but it seemed as if the added protection would be appreciated. They aren't running off their weight and have become round, soft, and full. I always pick them up when I pass through the stanchions, hold them close to my face so they will know me. They too shall stay with me forever.

It is not possible to separate these moments, one from another, into light and dark. It is not possible even to separate these moments into good or bad. Sometimes it isn't even possible to stand living them.

ANIMAL STORIES

I N HONOR of an effort to make a daily improvement in the barn, I reinstalled one of the original windows near the sheep stanchions this afternoon. It doesn't fit exactly but shall soon. Doing so cast a fine amount of light into the pen where the stanchions are. In the pen are Jenny and the twins; a first-time lamber who was a gift to me with her little ram, the one she loves to hate; and another first-time lamber that I had assisted in giving birth a couple of weeks ago. I had heard her crying over the baby monitor, went down, and saw an incorrect presentation. Head, no feet. I promptly penned her in one of the new jugs, pulled the lamb, and put it next to her. He was alive, microscopically small, couldn't stand. I didn't fight to save him. If he were tough enough to make it, then it would be remarkable. If not, he'd not be worth fighting for. This was the first time I'd made such a decision. But the ewe was only a year old. It was her first baby, she'll have many more, and I'd had enough of bottle lambs to last me the season. I found him dead in the morning. She had a nice udder, so I decided to stanchion her and try to graft a lamb or two onto her. It made her, however, absolutely frantic, and I chose not to force a lamb on her on the off chance that she'd supplement one of the three lambs remaining there. She didn't.

I was working in the aisle, pleased with the new window, when I heard a different kind of conversation among the ewes in the pen than I was accustomed to hearing. The new window with its nine lights brightened the area in a joyful kind of way. And there was the ewe lamb, the one who had lost her baby, cleaning a large sturdy ram lamb. His skin was wet and shiny with the bright yellow gleam that covers lambs that have been born under stress. I took the twins and lamb who was now in occupancy in the lambing jug back to the stanchion pen and brought the sturdy little guy who had just been born back to the jug where his mother gave birth two weeks ago to his brother. I then opened the stanchion pen gate. She leaped out, made a beeline to the jug where she had spent so difficult a day two weeks go, climbed in, and settled down with the little new ram. Oh, how pleased she is. This is the second time in eleven years that I've had a ewe freshen twice in two weeks. A hormonal accident.

There is a lamb about which I'd love to write a story one day. She is the tiniest lamb who ever survived here. Her mother is, herself, a lamb. The fifth of the lambing pens is only partially built. There is a light hanging above it, as well as the baby monitor. Her dam climbed into the partially built pen and proceeded to freshen, cleaned her lamb all by herself, and began to nurse that tiny, tiny little thing. Perfectly.

I came down from the house after hearing her arrival into the world. I picked her up. She was so light in my hand that she felt like a puff of cotton candy. Over the past couple of days I've been picking her up often. Every time I pass her. Sometimes I am just looking for an excuse to hold her. She is a wonder. This afternoon I let her dam outside for water. The lamb looked everywhere for her, to no avail. Then, suddenly sighting me, she ran up and stood still, only after positioning herself firmly on my boot. But I had to do my chores. I picked her up once more and put her down in a safe place. Not safe enough for her. Soon I noticed a pair of dark eyes staring at me. She had climbed into a small compartment in a grain feeder and was watching my every movement. She neither moved nor took her eyes off of me until I let her mother back inside. This little one has a mind, I kept thinking. And she shall stay here forever.

This is the story of how Rose Red Abernathy saved her mother's life. I was determined to start culling sheep this year for the first time. There are some ewes that just aren't doing well and some rams left over from last year. The latter would have to go, of course. And while the ewes lack of performance was a certainty, I've always offered my sheep a second chance. This year's incredibly high hay prices were an added incentive. My decisions about choosing which lambs I keep and how I manage this farm are often emotional ones. I try to choose lambs based on how I think they will perform, but sometimes a lamb will stay because she is the smartest or has a personality or curls up in my lap. As did one today.

I couldn't resist Snow White and Rose Red, the Abernathy sisters. They were both a practical and an emotional choice. Their dam is one of my oldest sheep and gave me a regular set of twins each year for the past eight. But this year and last she was unable to nurse her lambs. I decided she should go. Snow White and Rose Red have spent a couple of weeks in the house after their adventure of having been rescued from a snowbank, buried moments after their birth, but when the time came, they adjusted nicely to the lamb bar in the barn. They accost the milk with vigor and enthusiasm that are unsurpassed by any of their cousins or half brothers and sisters.

The other day, I filled the milk pail and went about my chores. It is always clear when the bottle lambs have finished. They tend to lie down in a heap on a pile of straw and take a nap. I heard a familiar voice. And there, in front of one of the piles, looking up was Rose Red Abernathy. I sat down on the floor. Rose Red climbed into my lap and put her head against me. She snuggled into my arms. Her mother Amanda had thrown a very wise little lamb. Amanda shall stay.

Giuseppe Nunzio Patrick MacGuire has spent the coldest part of the winter living in the lambing room, quite alone. The original plan was to repair one of the stalls in the carriage house, but that has yet to happen. He sometimes has been known to chase the sheep out of his paddock. And lambs have made him nervous. It has been a major undertaking to keep them from running into the lambing room when I go in to water and feed him. Gradually I realized I wasn't talking to him very often. Rarely did I put my arms around his neck. He had become an afterthought. Oh, have I watered Nunzio? And so I decided to take a chance and bring him into the aisle of the barn.

Two gates divide the aisle now. It would seem to be possible to keep him separate from the lamb bar. I went down the ladder with very mixed feelings. Am I going to create more problems for myself? The aisle is where I drop hay and do my chores. Will Nunzio interfere? There he was. He had opened the latch from the lambing room and was standing in the aisle. He was eating a little corn left from the lambs' last evening's dinner. He looked a little worse for wear. My heart went out to him. He promptly put his head under my arm. I wrapped my arms around his neck.

The marmalade barn cats, Prescott and Prentice, have been living in the cellar of the house during these deep snows and cold weather. I put them out a few days ago when the thermometer balanced at thirty degrees. They returned to their real home, the barn, immediately. Lambs love cats. They rub their faces along the length of the two orange cats from the tip of their noses to the tip of their tails. The cats love it. It is a delight to watch. The roosters have also decided to move into the barn along with some of the summer's new chickens. I was filling the mangers with hay when something made me look up. The barn was filled with sheep and lambs. Prentice and Prescott were sitting on the old stanchions. The roosters, green and gold, black and orange, were perched on brackets. Nunzio was standing, his head over a gate, his bridle a tomato red. Suddenly it all felt so very right. It was right for us all to be there together. Balanced perfectly. Something I didn't realize was missing was now there, Nunzio was the biggest part of it. But Prescott and Prentice counted as well. And the roosters. Suddenly it felt more than perfect. It felt like fairyland.

THE GIFT

T IPPY HEDRON is dying. Slowly. She doesn't want to. She is a sheep whom I always think of as young but is, in fact, old. Just as I think my dog Samantha is only four years old but is, in fact, going to be eight on Thanksgiving. Tippy Hedron has separated herself from the flock a great deal this summer. I'd come across her on the side hill from time to time, or looking into the pasture, Wuthering Heights, when the other sheep were inside. Of late, she has been coming near me asking to be petted every time I am amidst the flock.

A couple of days ago I saw a single ewe in Wuthering Heights. It seemed odd to me. As I also wanted to check the amount of water in the runoff up there. I went across the brook and on up to the field. While the sheep I had seen from the dining room window appeared to be standing, by the time I arrived, she was down. The rock she was lying on was warm from the sun. I couldn't lift her to her feet and had to drag her to the softer earth. I bit off small pieces of the two apples in my pocket and fed them to her. She ate voraciously. I pulled some thick green grass, which she also ate quickly. I then went back to the house, drew a couple of gallons of water, got some second-cutting hay, and went back up the side hill. She was more hungry than thirsty but ate and drank with a serious determination. There was no way to bring her down to the barn. It seemed best to leave her. I sat with her for a while, and then, in the dying light, went back down the hill, home.

The rains came that night. I woke to the sound of them. Guilt ridden and full of despair, I stayed awake all night at the thought of Tippy alone in the dark, pelted by the heavy rain. I fell asleep at dawn and woke two hours later. The brook was high for the first time since the beavers left. I was certain she had died in the night. I waited for my workman to come to help me bury the sheep. The brook was too high to cross in the pickup, so I went, with dread in my heart, alone up to Wuthering Heights. The sheep was nowhere in my line of vision. The gate was open. I went in. And there was the expectant, eager face of Tippy Hedron looking up at me once again. She tried to stand and could not. I moved her, trying to position her more comfortably, filled her water bowl from the water jugs I had left behind, and ran back for some more of the second-cutting hay I had fed her the day before.

She is going to die. She is older than the age when most sheep are either culled (sent to the auction to be bought for dog food) or die from accidental or natural causes. My sheep live far longer and continue to breed older than most. Knowing all of this, it remains almost unbearable to lose one.

This morning I shall go across the brook and up the hill once more. Do I carry an apple or two in my pocket and a flake of hay in my arms? Do I risk the despair of leaving it there upon finding her dead? Or do I go up empty-handed and risk nothing of my heart, most willing to race back to the barn for some more second cutting, should she still live, to buy one more day for her? Do I anticipate heartbreak and live with it ten minutes sooner than need be, or do I dare hope knowing that said hope may be dashed? The choice shall be made from either the place in my heart that has been worn down by experience, or the place in my heart that has held a lamb in my arms in the rocking chair in the kitchen, wintertime lambing, until it shows life or dies. On this most glorious of September mornings, which shall it be? Or rather, who am I, Tippy Hedron? Who have I become?

I have tossed away a commitment to the following of lists, of things to do, if not the actual lists themselves. It is a high-risk departure in this

September of all Septembers. Never before have I been so close to the possibility of being able to manage this farm as I am now. Some built-in pressures have become alleviated, and some other conditions have improved modestly, but improved nonetheless. The one thing I cannot stand, however, at the moment, is the tyranny of those lists. They were once a statement of my ability to control and anticipate order. They are now a prison from which I only can wish to escape. And so, for the moment, I can only follow my instincts as to what I do with my day. And the load is gradually lightening.

Yesterday was spent in sheer self-indulgence. What does that mean to this farmer? It means that the man who works for me came yesterday, did miscellaneous little things rather than big, serious, and obviously needed things. I had him cut up a downed apple tree for the Christmas fire and some pine branches for my French ceramic stove, the one that calls for hot-burning wood, pine or thorn apple. I painted the far side of a gate and a drop latch on another smaller gate that was left unpainted for both the lack of paint and the knowledge that only I could see the unpainted side. Ernest rebuilt a sawhorse I put down by the brook in which to cut up the kindling the beavers created when building their dam. He cut down a branch from the maple tree that obscured the view of the house from the road and in doing so caused said maple to appear to spread itself above and around the house in a broad embrace. An orange sign by the roadside announcing children at play was removed, since the children who played are no longer children. Some willow cut down a year ago was tied and brought to the wood room. And in all manner of things, details were arranged in ways creating order in my mind and took away, quietly, some of the pressure I live with every day. I think, when the pressures of life are so urgent, that it becomes necessary to lose sight of who one is as a way to protect oneself. But it is that personal self that provides solutions and a dimension of being without which one does not survive. Therein lies the dilemma.

I realized something the other day about writing stories for the county newspaper. I realized that they are the only way that people here in the town where I live have ever been able to get to know me. Oh, I have, as everyone does in a small town, a reputation. Partially true, partially false, and partially a creation of the minds of the story-tellers. I have heard, of course, much of the unflattering aspects of what people think of me and, as human nature usually dictates, very little of any positive aspects of my reputation. The world knows I am poor, certainly. That is obvious. And, in being so, have some of the problems that most people do when survival is the key issue of their lives. However, because I have never actually integrated into the life in the village, or even the lives of my neighbors on the Creek, I have rarely had the opportunity to give to the community what my nature would wish. Some efforts have been rebuffed and others received in the spirit in which I intended. But I have rarely had the ability to give what I would really like to give, except in the weekly writing over the past eight years of the stories of the farm. There are several threads that I understand to be common throughout them all. And those threads are what I perceive to be the gift. I stand here on this farm, alone of course, but not quiet. Over a hundred sheep, two dogs, one donkey, one barn cat, three geese, one heifer, and a multiple of roosters and chickens disqualify me from considering myself to be absolutely alone, but it is to be understood what I mean. And that gift is the demonstration that it is possible, no matter how hopeless one's life may seem or how im-possibly difficult a situation, or how much of a sense of failure one's heart can absorb, it is possible absolutely, without qualification, to hold on to one's dream. Never, no matter what the circumstances, to let it go. If that can be my gift, it is the very best I have to give.

FEBRUARY DAYS,
FEBRUARY NIGHTS

F EBRUARY, AND all I have ever known it to mean, brings with it a touch of dread to the mornings. Every day I steel myself to face the thermometer reading in the kitchen. With any luck the first number to greet me will be a sturdy forty-four degrees. Inside. And a pleasant twenty-two degrees outside. The only comfort in seeing forty-four degrees inside is the memory of my handwriting on a page one July morning. I had written: "kitchen 42 degrees, 6 A.M." Last night the weather created an accident. Cold descended upon this farm with a ferocity of speed that I have rarely seen. I had prepared some bottles and went to the barn to feed out hay and the bottle lambs. It was nearly dark. By the time I got from my kitchen to the barn door, my hands were locked with cold. My fingers froze onto the metal door latch. And downstairs my hand froze once again to my hay knife. I did my best in the barn, not good enough, and ran back to the house. The water had frozen in the front bathroom where it had been running quite nicely two hours before. The temperature was zero on the outdoor thermo-meter. The motor in the washing machine had frozen. Again. I did all of the things that one does, experience born of desperation, and waited. Then I did all of the things once more and waited. By eleven o'clock at night, I had stabilized the life here and went to bed.

In the morning the outdoor thermometer read thirty. The indoor thermometers read thirty-two in the living room, thirty-four in the kitchen. I've never seen so small a gap between the two before. The washing machine intake had thawed and the machine had run sometime in the night, but the drain is positioned in an unenviable spot and was, therefore, still frozen. The laundry still sits, soaking, in cold and dirty water. I'll hang it to drip in the basement and then hang it to dry in the kitchen. I have an Excedrin headache. A rare occurrence, but nonetheless I have one now.

Of all the things I have learned living here, one of the most important is that in February the washing machine must be made to work. And in order to achieve a state beyond that of simply surviving, a virtue unto itself, details must not be ignored. Clean curtains in this wood-heated house, and tablecloths starched to within an inch of their lives, and scrubbed kitchen tiles all contribute to the sharpness of mind and eye that will help me keep my livestock in the best health and state of well-being. I become error prone in February and misstep on occasion. I do know how to avoid the dangers midwinter affords, but the line is a fine one. Carefully drawn. I must use all of what I know not to cross it.

It is a fortunate thing indeed to be blessed with this farm and all of the abundance and joy that its creation, maintenance, and possibilities afford. It is also a fortunate thing to have been able to apply who I am and who I have become to this farm, because in no other situation would I have been able to play out so many sides of myself. While I am an imperfect farmer, lacking the instincts and experience that ultimately make one that in the truest sense, other gifts that I have to offer have served us well. And my farm shows that. It is unique unto itself, its own kind of place, with its own spirit and vitality. I am glad of that. The issue at hand, however, is how best to husband us all using our strengths to overcome our weaknesses in this intensely treacherous month.

February is a month when books are of great importance to me. I need to get away, cabin fever, and nothing has the power to take me away as much as what one finds on the pages of a book. Unfortunately, I am a fast reader. Equally unfortunately, it is only a certain kind of book that will do. There must be a variety of visual images, preferably of another country, England or France will do quite nicely. There should be some smells of fine food as well, imagined, of course, possibly to be recreated in my own kitchen. Simenon does that best in his Maigret series, as Superintendent Maigret loves to eat, and the stories always include some detailed and memorable descriptions of French cooking. I do recreate some of it on my wood stove, to enjoy while reading. If I am lucky, I will find a nice autobiography to provide a distancing from the sameness of days that February affords in such great abundance. *The Horse of Pride*, about a village in Brittany, served me well, as did my newly discovered *A Country Woman in Twentieth-Century France* (which, by the way, would have been more appealing had it retained its original title, translated from the French, *A Soup of Wild Herbs*).

I read mystery books not for any interest in the mystery itself; I rarely figure out in advance, nor do I care, who done it. What I love is the variety of people who are introduced into my evenings when I am curled up in my tidy green chair in front of the living room fire, after the lambs have gone to bed, and the countrysides, all of them, float back and forth in my mind's eye. Michael Innis makes me want to read with a dictionary at my side, or at least a pad and pencil. While I understand of what he is speaking, I don't even recognize some of his vocabulary and find myself searching his words for their Latin roots. The joy of English mystery writers with classical educations.

There is a downside to all of this mental extravagance: the blurred edges of housekeeping in both of the houses here, mine and that of the sheep. The abrupt turn of the last page of a book brings my eye to the upswept hearth, or the crumbs on a tablecloth. Do I spend the hot water on the washing of saucers or washing of tablecloths? Is there any bread left from Saturday's baking or, better yet, some coconut Danish? Do I bring in the remaining firewood left outside or sweep the barn? Which gives me away. I've been known to finish a book in the early hours of morning rather than begin my chores immediately. If there is disorder when I return from these journeys to France or England, or total immersion in a book about the history of mathematics, the benefits of travel are lost, as I become depressed and as overwhelmed proportionately as I was distanced from reality.

Nonetheless, in the day, when all of the externals of life were dissected into a costs-and-anticipated-time-involved-to-achieve list, there were two things which appeared with punctuality on the list of ways best to survive and even enjoy February. Good chocolate and good books. In those days I didn't mention a washing machine or a variety of brooms all appropriate to the occasion of use: barn brooms, house brooms, cellar brooms. Christmas this year afforded me good chocolate in an astonishment of variety. Justina, having become a pastry chef, now knows how to make chocolates. And what incredible chocolates they are. The rest of the family bought me a most generous supply of bittersweet Lindt bars. And I've rediscovered the Rose and Laurel Bookstore, in Oneonta, where I've been buying some books for a dollar or two on my weekly grain run. Which, I must admit, is an excuse for having lunch at Sweet Indulgence, always a restauratif for the body and soul, in addition to being the finest food in Oneonta. That, too, takes me away, to an Italian kitchen with the textures and flavors of a home-cooked delight.

What I need most today is the self-discipline to wax the kitchen floor and iron the tablecloths so I won't become guilt ridden upon emerging from a book for an hour or two of running away from home. The haymow floors are swept and in order, no guilt to be found there. Discipline may be afforded by the momentary absence in the house of a book unread or a story to be written. February days, February nights.

THE SILENT RHYTHM OF THE DAYS

MISS CLARA Peggittee, doe goat on this sheep farm, has begun to bag. So why is it such a surprise? February 15th has floated around in my mind as her due date for quite some time. But also, in quite the incorrect time slot, has been the date August 15th, to designate when she was covered. The day I thought the pygmy buck arrived. She went into heat immediately upon seeing him. He covered her a few minutes later. She is not "showing" any signs of having a kid in the near offing. And that is in itself scary. I'm not sure if it is simply because she is carrying a pygmy type goat like the buck rather than a too small LaMancha like herself.

One of the things that amazes me the most about farming is how immediate solutions to long-pressing problems present themselves when it is absolutely necessary. Eleventh-hour solutions. I've not known where to put the goat should she freshen. The obvious stall in the carriage house needs be mucked out and my extra time recently has been spent making the barn ready for new hay, not in the carriage house readying for a kid. I've bought some very nice round bales that have been wrapped in an onion bag kind of plastic mesh, resulting in nearly perfect hay. Less than an inch of the outer layer of the wheel is spoiled. The rest is sweet and very beautiful first cutting. I'd like to be able to roll the bales out on the barn floor and rake the hay onto a tarp to carry out to the sheep. The carriage house was most thoroughly trashed by the flock this winter, and while cleaning it again shall be interesting, some of the other details in the lambing room and barn have proved to be more interesting. Therefore, I've been in attendance, with greater regularity, in the barn.

And so this afternoon when I noticed Miss Peggittee's bag once again, I decided to check it. It was full. But she appears not to be. I went into the newly ordered upper level of the barn and made a wall of bales of second cutting, put a piece of plywood against another wall in between it and a long ladder lying on its edge to hold the plywood against the battenless bridgeway wall, pulled out a long portable fence and used that as the hypotenuse of the right triangle, tying it on one end to the ladder. I put more bales of hay to brace it and keep the drafts away. Suddenly, there was, in deep clean litter, a small but adequate draftfree pen for the goat. She is bedded down in it now. It's not the roomiest stall in the barn, but it is quite cozy and nice, and she seems more content than I have seen her in a long time.

My lambing room is functioning at last, for bottle lambs and a mother whose smallest of twins can't manage to hang on long enough to get enough milk. It is a pleasure to go down there. Lambs are fickle creaturers, racing madly from one delight to the next. New hay. Hooray. Cracked corn. Hooray. Lamb feed. Hooray. A bucket of warm water. Hooray. This morning's hay fluffed up again. Hooray. The grain shook up a little. Hooray. They dashed every-where, especially to wherever they see someone else, stopping short to stare up at me for bottles. Even the ones who were weaned a few weeks ago. Oh, knock that guy down, grab that bottle. Hooray. I fluff hay, redistribute grain, bottle, give warm water, or something, it would seem, all day long. And each time I'm down there they act as if whatever is being done for them is the most exciting thing in the world. And it is. Even when I open or close the shutters or put a chicken into the nesting box, excitement runs high.

Little Molly Malone is down there, getting bigger and brighter every day. She is a pretty little fluffy thing, with black eyes and the soft cocoa spot that characterizes the lambs I'm keeping for myself this year. The newly named Thumbilina also shall stay, daughter of Brunhilda, sheep terrible. Thumbilina has learned the merits of sitting quietly in my lap and allowing herself to fall asleep. Her dam has calmed down considerably and even came near me without trying to ram me into the ground.

I have not been concentrating on which I shall be keeping this year, except for those lambs who have been born with the thick curly fleece and a cocoa-colored spot on the back of their neck. There are about sixteen of them now, maybe seventeen. Two, who came close to specification, are living at a friend's. And of the rest, six ewes are here. The first years of the cocoa-spotted lambs provided only ram lambs. This year were the first ewes and the greatest number of lambs with these characteristics. The lambs usually have one bent ear, the right, which sometimes but not always remains bent, a remarkably soft thick wavy fleece, a cocoa-colored spot on the back or back of the neck, black hooves, and a squarish head, and are very, very pretty. They are perfect I think for this farm. Lambs who are born walking and talking (their dams have been fed haylage) and have thick fleeces to brave the winter are already three steps ahead of the crowd.

The other thing that amazes me about farming is the never-ending wellspring of hope that comes from nowhere, or rather, could seem to come only from the hand of God, a hope that springs forth with a purity and joy and resourcefulness absolutely without warning at totally unexpected moments. This farm is in a dramatically drastic position. One of my jobs ended in November. My tenants moved out a few weeks ago, owing two months' rent. The bank is breathing down my neck for a mortgage payment. Late, per usual. It is remarkably warm outside so I didn't make a fire in the living room, where I sit writing. After all, it's been fifty-two degrees here before with the fire blazing. Why waste the wood?

And yet all I am thinking about is the goat freshening, a possible new cow arriving, the neatly packaged round bales, and choosing which lambs to keep and how to fence them. In my mind's eye I saw my prettiest pasture, by the road, with the dark green outdoor chicken coop and some black and white hens, a new portable coop for the goslings, Toulouse again, to be bought late spring, and a half a dozen or so pretty lambs racing around inside the dark green wooden fences with all of the world driving by to see. And my spirits lift on shining wings with the question to be asked of my helper when he arrives next about what kind of fencing to add to keep the appropriate stock in and appropriate stock out.

Snow stares at me from a distant hill. The rattle of the electric heater in the basement reminds me to run downstairs to turn it off. Every penny counts here at the moment. My coffee is cold. I haven't washed my face yet. The living room floor begs to be mopped and polished. In other words, things are a bit grungy here for the moment. But my stock has been fed and my heart is full of joy at the thought of putting up still another few hundred feet of fence in which to keep the new young Greenleaf breed of sheep. To me, it is that astonishing wellspring of hope and joy that is the essence of farming. The thought of what will happen next when this farmer does this or that or the other thing. Despair has not entered. And the silent rhythm of the days rolls on, each day bringing its own beauty.

A REMARKABLE WOMAN

M Y MOTHER was a remarkable woman. All of us, I've come to understand, are the amazing products of varying degrees of appropriate parenting that we received. Some parents "doing their best" were not to be good enough. Some were too good. My mother's mothering was famous. It was famous for the overprotective aspect, not of her nature but of her experience. Her nature was determined, strong, forceful, and profoundly loving. However, tragedy bound itself to those qualities, therefore she overprotected me in ways most complicated.

While we never fully know our parents, time most gradually unfolds our understanding and our experience of them, myth blends with reality, and the reality of who we are enlightens us about them.

I read recently an article about some, and I'm glad it is only some, women writers who struggle with issues of creativity. These few seem to blame their mothers for their problems. Some resort to psychotherapy, others to support groups "to work out issues about wanting to be creative." My first response to reading about such people is to want to shake them and shout into their ears, "Wake up!" My next is to feel horrified at being so judgmental. My third is to want to tell them to get a job, a real job, milking cows or in a factory somewhere, or force-feeding ducks, a job that will make you so tired you can't think.

I know that when I was in my thirties I spent a lot of time complaining about what my mother hadn't done for me. One cousin, Norma, said of my mother, her aunt, "She did the best she could," and I retorted, "It wasn't good enough." I was wrong. It certainly was good enough. I now understand that the grand mix of "not good enough" and "good enough" is what has helped create the person I am and am always in the process of becoming. If some of those poor souls in the newspaper article had parents who interfered with their creativity, I should only feel sorry for them. My mother, who was herself without a tiny bit of creativity in her nature, had only admiration for what she saw as creativity in me. "She's creative," she'd say, drawing out the word to the magnitude that three syllables can afford, emphasis on the "a" every time. On the other hand, she never thought to provide me with any of the materials that would have helped creativity bloom. So be it. I had to do it myself. I still do. And I'm glad of it. When I ran out of paper on which to draw, I drew pictures with crayons on the windows of my room, making "stained glass." My mother, a very tidy housekeeper, didn't mind. "She's creative," she said.

I used to complain when I was nine about being told to draw on the back of typing paper I used as art paper, if I ran out of it. Years later she apologized. She just didn't understand, she said. How could she have? She didn't have a doll to play with until she was five or six, and then made her own. She took it to the show her grandmother, who had been a wealthy woman once and knew of store-bought things, who said to her, "You call that a doll?" My mother threw it away and never had a doll again.

She told me that story when she was eighty years old. "And don't you go make me a doll," she said. "It will only make me cry." I didn't. I wanted to so badly, but I didn't want to make her cry. This winter, when some hurtful things happened to me, I decided that whenever I am deeply hurt by someone, I will make a doll to give to a child whom I don't know. I wasn't thinking of my mother at the time, only of what would make my sadness go away. To give a child who didn't have one a beautiful handmade doll. Yet my mother named me after her grandmother. Almost all things in life are multifaceted. We carry with us threads and ribbons of so many different colors, weights, and textures. It is amazing we are ever one thing. And who I am is, in some parts, a great-grandmother I never saw and my mother in ways I may never understand.

I am a farmer. It is a matter of great pride to me to call myself that. I never call myself a writer. In part it is because in our society to be a writer is often considered being a special person. It is a highly overrated evaluation, in my opinion. I think being a farmer is being a special person. I, and other farmers, feed people. Without farmers we'd all starve. Being a writer feeds the heart and soul, of course, and it provides grain for my chickens, cow, and donkey every Wednesday when I cash my check from writing a story for the local newspaper.

I don't wish to say writing has no value. But I know its claim to the quality of being creative is grossly exaggerated. Creativity lies in all human endeavors. Washing my cow's udder and getting it right at last is the height of creativity to this farmer who also writes stories. And hitting the pail just right to make sweet, thick foam is fabulously creative to me. And making cheese, and planning new fence, and looking for a calf, and finding the right basket for collecting eggs, and making a nest for the geese, and braiding a halter for the cow all give me a deep sense of satisfaction.

When I bought this land and this twenty-five-room house, I told everyone who would listen that it is an endless palette for me. And now, remembering the window I drew on when I was nine, I realized I bought a house with sixty-five windows to draw on, or to sew curtains for through which to frame a view. To define creativity as only an art form is too narrow a scope to satisfy the meaning of the word.

My grandfather was a farmer out of necessity, but I've never been sure if he liked it or had an affinity for it. My mother was very poor as a child, and except for a period in her marriage before my father became too sick to run his business any longer, she never had very much in the way of money and material goods, but she felt my brother and I were her treasures, and the poverty of her childhood never affected her sense of self-worth. She was Rose. And that was that.

I noticed the poverty that my brother and I were raised with, but it was a far different kind from that which my mother knew. We had an abundance of food, warm clothes, love, and attention. It never oppressed me, and I had only a sense of pride from learning to make do. And so I've created a lifestyle in which, while I am cash poor, I am materially wealthy. After all, I own one milking cow, one heifer, and one calf. I have a donkey. I have a summer bedroom and a winter bedroom. Never mind that the summer bedroom is a bit too cold in which to sleep in the winter (the winter bedroom can be as well, but I won't think about that). To have two bedrooms from which to choose in the same house, that is wealth.

My mother was raised on a farm in Niantic making me, in fact, a Connecticut Yankee. She was the middle child of seven, the first to finish eighth grade. Children went to work at a very young age in rural communities, to work in the mill or at the local factory. When she graduated eighth grade and was asked if she was to go now to the mill, she said no and went to a two-year high school. When asked again to go to the mill, she said no and traveled many miles to go to a high school that graduated students from a four-year program. There were two high schools from which to choose, one was Chapman Tech, a vocational school, the other Williams Memorial Institute, a middle-class girls' high school. She chose Williams. She refused once more to work in the mill upon graduation from high school and was filled with guilt. She had not made a contribution to her family's well-being while her older sisters and brother had already made their sacrifices. She turned down a scholarship to a four-year college, accepted one to the shorter-termed Yale Normal School, and became a teacher. She taught in a one-room rural schoolhouse encompassing eight grades. Some of the boys in her school were eighteen years old and six-foot-tall farm boys. My mother was a tiny five foot two inches tall. She gave all of her salary to her father for the first year and a half of working. One day she went to New London, cashed her paycheck, and purchased a "store-bought" outfit to wear to work. She told me my grandfather said nothing to her when she brought the reduced salary to him.

She raised me with a fierce determination. She believed that being a mother to me and my bother was an absolute commitment, unwavering in dedication and intensity. She believed I could do anything I wanted to do. She insisted on that belief. And so I am always surprised when I fall short of the belief she held with such consistency. One of the things I am so grateful to her for is that I have an absolute unrestricted freedom in my life in regard to the elusive and treacherous realm called creativity. If, indeed, our mothers hold such a powerful sway over that part of us then she certainly gave me a remarkable gift. A remarkable gift from a remarkable woman.

THE HAWK

TIME IS slipping by with an increasing urgency. I've started this story in many ways and discarded them all. And now it must be written through to completion and I don't know how to do it. The events that have shattered our security in this country continue to have their repercussions. As they shall forever. They affect us all in ways both small and large, in ways measurable and not, each of us reacting in our own individual style.

I find that my days have a clarity that I have not experienced since I first lived here, and I was wrapped in a sense of adventure, gilded with hope and promise. Each moment has its own shining beauty, and I see with a sharpened focus that it is new and unadorned. To live with fear is not an unusual state of mind for me. But that fear has been altered to include all of us, all Americans everywhere. And, God help them, the innocent of other countries who, by the sheer accident of being in the wrong place at the wrong time, shall also soon die. Casualties of a war. Each day holds its own reminder that it must be lived in its fullest. And one must be, in oneself, a better person living it than the day before.

I think of my friends and family, some of whom may even find it necessary to live here on my farm. What in myself needs to change to get along with so independent a group of individuals? How shall I cook? My children are accustomed to the now very old-fashioned French country food that I have always made. But what of my brother who is not? And my late husband's sister? Familiar food is so essential to morale. How would someone feel never to get to eat things one enjoys the most. Would I give up my tyranny over the stove? What must I do to learn how not always to be the boss?

September has been so very beautiful this year. Clear skies, rare in Delaware County, have been a gift to us. As were the skies, I read over and over again in Angela Thirkell's novels, most beautiful over England the first year of the Second World War. But it is our obligation to enjoy all of the beauty that we are given in each moment and not succumb to the fear the terrorists so absolutely wish to instill. Stories still come every day from the city. It is not over. And may never be. But we must go forward.

I have put the sheep in the barn for the past several days now. They had been on the move. Once or twice, no matter what my effort had been, they managed to get themselves out. Rotational grazing the neighbor's pastures. His cows have been roaming as well. Newcomers to the road think the cows are mine and stop to tell me, "Your black cows are out." Which makes me laugh. Those magnificent creatures are not mine. Nor would I know what to do with them if they were. They siphon up grass and turn it into meat while my Jersey Lady Annabella Pilkingston siphons up ten pounds of grain a day and is losing condition as she nurses her calf. I like milk cows. The monstrous Angus are just not my style.

I went to Chamber's Auction in Unadilla last Wednesday to sell my old favorite ram, William Fitzwilliams. It is not my habit to stay to watch the sale. I don't care to see my carefully raised livestock frightened in the show ring. This time was different. A friend has expressed interest in owning some laying hens and a Nubian goat or two to milk. It was more important to find her a goat than mourn my ram.

The style of bidding changed for a brief second during the rabbit, chicken, goose, duck, rooster-selling event. The custom is to show one of the animals being sold out of the box or cage, to indicate what the others look like. I didn't take my eye off of the cage of chickens I would have bought for Jennifer when suddenly to my amazement it was walked out of the door. That cage was sold only by number; they didn't pull a chicken out of it first. I missed it. We then came to a family of kid goats. Some were very pricey. And I hoped they were not going for meat. The tiny one I liked the best went as part of a buy-three-at-the-price deal. I asked a person next to me to include her in his bid. But the lot went up higher than his limit. It was too high for him. I was outbid. When I went to pay my bill I saw the woman who had bought the little goat. "You are not going to eat her, are you?" I asked.

"No, she is for my child," was the reply. And so the pretty little kid went to a family to be a pet. I was so relieved.

A huge old basket had gone up for sale. It is rare, these days, that I ever buy anything just because I like it. But I did like that basket very much. It had shoulder straps and was in fact a huge backpack, a very nice one at that. I had a limit on what I was willing to spend. Went ten dollars over it. The bidding was fast, very fast. In two-dollar-and-fifty-cent increments I'm not used to. I gave up. And suddenly found the auctioneer saying to me, "Lady, do you want it?" For five dollars over my "ten dollars over my limit."

"Yes," I said. They passed it back to me. "You'll never be able to carry that," went up a chorus all around me. "What you're going to put in it, anyway?"

"I certainly can," I replied to the first chorus. "Apples," to the second. I've become obsessed with apples of late. Picking and sorting all manner of varieties. Each type is becoming part of an experiment. Which can store throughout the winter? Which can best be made into a pie? Which makes the old-fashioned apple cheese? And which the best glazed apples? I already know the preferred kind for sauce.

And so I walked out at the end of the auction with a check in my pocket from the sale of my ram, the pack on my back, and neither the kid goat nor the chickens. So be it.

I did a million errands in Oneonta that day, with an atypical resolve. It is rare that I push Ernest beyond what he considers acceptable, but this time I did. I went to the *Oneonta Star* to place an ad for an apartment I have to rent. I bought lath with which to make racks for apples for my newly appreciated root cellar and odds and ends of hardware to take the edge off discomfort here. With dispatch.

I came home to a calm and silent house, and stood in the living room to hear the messages on my answering machine. Ernest called me from the backyard. By name. He never does that. I ran outside. He had just killed a hawk. It had attacked and killed one of the baby chicks in the cage by the kitchen door. The mother hen was still alive. There were feathers everywhere. The hawk had been tangled in the mesh of the cage. Trapped. All of the other chicks were gone. Presumed dead. It was a beautiful and strange wild thing lying there. The dead hawk. Barely a sign of how it had died. Shocking in its immediacy and in its closeness. I have always kept the chicken cage near the kitchen door. The chicks come and go at will. The hen calls warning to them. This time her chick wasn't fast enough. I usually have a roof on the cage. This time I didn't. The hawk must have seen it from very high up in the sky. How strange it all is. Later that evening I went outside and spoke to Celeste Baldwin, my goat. I had let the hen loose but hadn't moved the dead chick or its cage. The hawk was lying on some hay. I wanted to examine it closer. At the sound of my voice, one at a time, each of the four baby chicks emerged and ran toward me.

PUNCTUATION MARKS

T HERE IS nothing in my life that makes me feel as privileged as to be a farmer. It numbers among the most fortunate experiences I have known to have so accidentally found my true vocation. Tomorrow shall mark a special event on this farm. Tomorrow five new lambs shall arrive. Half East Friesians. They are to be a jump start on the emerging dairy here. They are unrelated to my ram, which means they can be bred by him each year without concern and produce three-quarter East Friesian ewe and ram lambs. Were those to be bred back I shall have seven-eighths East Friesian sheep.

There are few experiences that are equal to the moment when new livestock arrives on a farm. I used to go with a trucker friend sometimes, a long time ago, as he brought newly purchased cows to a farm. The look on the farmer's face would be of cautious expectancy. Joy conservatively expressed. Hope shining in an unguarded moment. And, as suddenly, the mask of stoic normalcy resumed. No. The arrival of new stock was never an ordinary day.

In the morning after chores, his and mine, Ernest Westcott and I shall drive along Route 23 to Old Chatham, New York, on the first stage of this grand adventure to pick up some East Friesian ewe lambs, in his vanilla-colored pickup with burnt sienna lace on its skirts and the very nice livestock box on the top. And a grand adventure it shall be, particularly for the lambs who have been born and are being raised in a far different environment than ever shall be found here.

Snow dusts the pastures. The wind whips around the trees. I've let the chickens out of the portable coop to find their way to their old home in the carriage house. They did. Quickly. They have found where the cow spills some of her grain in the barnyard. And surround her. Cleaning it up to the last kernel of corn. My handyman thought poorly of me feeding Lady Annabella, my best cow, in a bucket so easy to tip over. But a container has never been made that she couldn't spill. She likes her lunch spread out. He watched her while building a new gate for the barnyard and grumbled all along about my wasteful cow, meaning my wasteful self. According to him, that is. "I wouldn't give it to her if she treats the bucket that way," he said again and again. "She's wasting it." "You wait," I replied. "There won't be a sign that there ever was any grain fed out there in a few minutes."

There wasn't. I was right and restrained myself from pointing it out. And so there is now a new gate to the barnyard. And miraculously enough built more closely to my specifications than things have been built of late. My gates are my pride and pleasure. This one is a copy of the very first one that was installed here. About twelve years ago. It was painted the willow green I love. Gradually it disintegrated as snowdrifts piled around it ruining the paint and sheep and cows battered it until they learned how to unlatch it. The next warmish day shall find it painted green. That very dark Charleston green that Harold in the paint store mixes so well for me. This year's gains were in tiny increments. As tiny as the gate. Some years have been more dramatic. But the year is not, as yet, over. And shall be punctuated by the arrival of the new lambs. Oh, the lambs shall need names. And ways to be identified. And bottles. And a place to live. And, perhaps, even their own notebook, if not a separate chapter in the history of the farm. I remember the second flock of great hope arriving a few years ago and the lovely names each had. Now to find some lovely ones for these. There is a beautiful and large apple crate in the upper level of the barn. I shall wrap plastic around its walls, stack bales of hay by its sides, and keep a sheet of plexiglas over it for protection from the night wind. The lambs shall live there. I hope.

Farmers are dreamers of the first order. The most romantic of dreamers. Feet in the soil, head in the clouds, backs bent even in today's tractors. They are most wishful of all of those who have inherited the earth as their legacy and work with their bodies as well as their minds. Who else depends so strongly on the unknown and goodwill of the unexpected as a farmer does? The impending birth of calves inspires dreams of the calf being the right calf. And growing into being the right cow. The planting, the haying, even the milking all being controlled by forces within the realm of knowledge and experience and yet controlled by a force far stronger than one can even begin to imagine. There are years when only steadfast grim concentration can carry one's step to the barn. And days when all goes so well that life is as close to perfection as is possible on this earth.

We are living in the center of a moment of great change. I've been reading history of late. With each such moment in history those living it believe that their moment is the most important and significant and dangerous. It then falls into place, along with all the others. As shall ours. There was an announcement a short time ago to expect another attack against our country. I called my children and my brother asking them to come here, in the hope that the countryside would be safe. They would not come. I told them how much I loved them. I played the Chopin piano sonatas that have been the only music that consoles me these days. Then I walked to the sink to wash dishes.

This could be my last day on earth, I thought. How many people in the passage of time have thought such a thought? And played their favorite music or sang their most favorite song while going about their appointed task. Because that was the only thing to do. And then faced their death. In all of the time that man has inhabited the earth, it has happened over and over again.

The rules for living are being rewritten on the farm. Some are new, but most are the same. Only now wearing quotation marks or exclamation points. Put the worst of the job to your back. Face only that which you have already accomplished. One cardinal rule: rather than shoveling the barn face forward, staring at the vast stretch before me, I turn my back to it and keep widening the place by the door, to see what is done rather than what is not.

And so I started cleaning the carriage house. In part, to rehouse the chickens for the winter. In part, to reorder the hay that was stacked in the loft. In part, in case I choose to use it for the new lambs when they outgrow the apple crate. The ground floor is awful. The loft, merely bad. With my back to the worst of it, I faced a wall and started stacking hay against it. I forked the loose hay into a manageable pile and bagged droppings from the chickens roosting on the rafters and the lambs and kid goats who shared the space from time to time. An hour, maybe two, away from being done. The chicken coop already has the nesting boxes clean and full of fluffy hay. Two Barred Plymouth Rocks have found their way back inside. Joy. Do I go so far as to clean the windows? I just might. I moved the pile of boards that I've been saving with which to make a box bed for the barn to sleep in when it is not possible to return to the house. And there were five eight-foot boards I don't remember buying. Planed on one side, rough on the other. Ten inches wide. I have wanted, for six years now, another set of bookshelves in the library. Ten inches wide.

Their presence is not yet a reward for cleaning the carriage house, because the carriage house is not clean. Their presence is about something else. A statement of fact. Of presence. Of being. Not a lesson to be learned. Lessons do not appeal to me. They have an artificial significance that fails to impress me for very long. But those long boards planed on one side, ten inches wide, have their own meaning. That pleases this Yankee farmer to no end.

LADY AGATHA VAN DER HORN

O N A S C A L E of one to ten, today measured a stout nine and three quarters on the misery quotient on the farm. Lady Agatha Van der Horn, red Jersey heifer, due to freshen this winter, pride of my heart, had disappeared, seemingly forever. Yesterday I realized I hadn't seen her since the evening before, or had it been the evening before that? I knew she had been in my next-door neighbor's cow path, a path unfrequented by any cow but mine for the past forty years. Nonetheless easily identifiable.

Time blends into itself, sometimes stretching to a vertical infinity in these hills and valleys. I started to keep an eye out for her. By late afternoon, I began to worry. She often turns up on the front lawn after breakfasting down the road. I went to the neighbor's cow path and found evidence of her having been there by the gate next to the road for some time. I followed her tracks to the bridge across the brook and took the most logical and straightforward route, as cows have a tendency to a logic not too dissimilar from that of human beings, a nice mowed path to my next-but-one neighbor's where she had been known to go. Drop apples on the lawn accounted for her predilection.

It is lovely there on the far side of the brook. I walked on to the back of Nina's yard. It is a glade of sorts, beautifully balanced plantings and nicely mowed lawn. No signs of the heifer having been recently in the vicinity. Evidences of cows' presences are usually unmistakable. The walk back was beautiful. The leaves are gone from the trees and I could see across the pond the white house next door as well as my farm from a fresh perspective.

Looking for a missing cow is, classically, one of a farmer's most deeply felt experiences. Looking for sheep is another matter entirely. Cows are a serious find. Sheep, well, sheep flock; therefore they are usually too numerous to miss. A single cow can sometimes blend into the landscape with the inherited instinct and inbred knowledge of the hunted. A missing cow usually wants to be a missing cow.

Barn boots have a distinctive sound. They have three separate notes as they hit the ground twice with each step and the foot once. The sound has been described as *kar rum ph. Kar rum ph.* My boots don't say *kar rum ph.* They say something else. What that something else is, exactly, eludes me. But speak they do, and so, while looking for Lady Agatha was making me feel increasingly sick at heart, the sound of those boots made me feel a part of a long line of people who have walked these hills for miles looking for a missing cow. I was in good company. It helped. But the sick feeling became increasingly overwhelming.

By the time evening was descending, I gave up and returned home. I was in a state I had experienced only when my first cows, Lady Francesca Cavadish and Dame Millicent Fallansbee, both wandering together, had disappeared. It is a special and distinctive kind of misery that extends from the center of the throat to the pit of the stomach. Dull. Insistent. As wide as it is deep. Despair tinged with hopelessness coated with guilt. Why, oh why, didn't I bring her in when I saw her last? Why did I think she'd come home by herself? The fact that she always did no longer mattered. This very special kind of misery is a heavy one. No tossing or turning all night here. No restless walking and falling back to sleep, just a heavy weight on the neck, chest, and stomach. It took hours of motionless staring into the darkness to fall asleep.

I woke up late, fully intending first to make the fires and have breakfast before going out to look once more for the cow, and proceeded instead to pull on a jacket and immediately run outside. I looked everywhere. In the barnyard, Lady Annabella Pilkingston, lead cow, was bellowing insistently. There was no answering bellow. Not that Lady Agatha ever answers. She is the least vocal cow I have ever owned.

Ernest pulled into the driveway. I jumped into the truck. We drove up and down the roads stopping at every farm that has cows. "Have you seen my cow?" Our eyes searched the hillsides. No manure to be seen on the roads. No errant heifer under an apple tree. Ernest looked to the left. I looked to the right. No sign of a cow.

"She couldn't have gone this far," he kept saying.

"My other cows have," I replied, my voice straining to find its way past the choking feeling around my throat.

We pulled into Buel's farm. I asked Ralph Buel had he seen my Jersey heifer. Ernest rolled down the window. "It isn't a Jersey. It's a red cow," he said.

"What are you talking about?" I shrieked above the sound of the radio, the static, and the truck's engine.

"It doesn't look like any Jersey I've ever seen," pronounced seventy years of cowmanship. "Jerseys are brown. This is a red cow you want. If you tell it is a Jersey, no one will know what you're talking about."

"She came from Wayne Bryden's farm. He had Jerseys, only Jerseys. With papers!" I yelled. All sense of the proper courtesy between myself and the people who work for me was thrust aside by fear and frustration. I didn't even try to score on the sore point of the distinction between heifers and cows. I've often been derided for referring to my animals by the incorrect designation. Ernest will always admonish me when I call Lady Agatha, all thousand pounds of her, equipped with horns big enough to defeat a tank, a cow. "She's a heifer until she freshens," he'll say. "And then she's a first-calf heifer. There's some who will still call her a heifer, even then. A second-calf heifer. Why, there's some that never even get a chance to be a called cow. They just stay on being a heifer. A third-calf heifer."

I insisted we drive the roads. "Just keep on going," I said.

"She isn't here," he replied. "If she were around she'd of come home," he said comfortingly, as all helping hands are wont to do.

"Are you saying someone took her?" I shouted.

"No, I am not saying anything," he replied.

"Right. Keep on driving. My other cows went here, once, up this road and around the bend."

I made him drive me everywhere a cow of mine has been known to go, except for Pete Hamilton's farm. I knew I'd never be believed that my cows had turned up there, eight miles from my farm as the crow flies.

We arrived home after an hour's search to hear Lady Annabella still bellowing in the barnyard. She had been locked in last night with her calf and all the sheep and the buck goat. I lock the barn door and latch the barnyard gates every evening after bringing the flock in for the night. Most of the sheep and both cows were in the barnyard eating hay. The only ones on pasture were the twenty or so who figured out how to scale a wall where once was a gate. My handyman kept repeating if she were around she'd have turned up by now. "Do you mean someone's taken her or that the coyotes have gotten her?" I asked.

"No, I'm not saying that."

"Then what are you saying?"

"I'm not saying anything."

I started to look for the tire tracks near the gate where I had last seen her, tried to remember if I had seen any cattle trucks come by that day, and broke down and asked what days were the sale days at the local auction. "Friday for calves and beefers. Monday's for heifers and cows." It was Saturday. She'd been last seen on Thursday evening. It became harder and harder to breathe. I tried to remember how long it took me to get over losing the last cow, the one that became blended into Tom Connelly's herd next door. No comfort there. I thought of calling the sheriff to ask if there could be a lookout for my heifer in the sale barn on Monday.

Ernest was to stay and work for another hour or two. It was hard to remember what else I needed done on this farm. All I could think of was the cow. But the cow getting out reminded me of what else is in the habit of getting out, and I asked him to fix the holes in the indoor chicken coop upstairs in the carriage house. The escape hatches they had made for themselves last spring had best be fixed before I enclose the chickens for the winter. He went out to the carriage house and on upstairs. I went down to the barn and opened the north side door to let the sheep out for the afternoon. I looked inside on the off chance Lady Agatha was there. No cow, only sheep. I went on through. Only Lady Annabella and her unnamed veal calf in the barnyard. I returned to the carriage house. Ernest said, "Look out the window. There's something unfamiliar in the barnyard." I looked. I counted. Three cows: Lady Annabella, the unnamed calf, and the bred heifer, Lady Agatha. She had come home. "She was always in there," said the voice of authority.

"Impossible. Not for three days. How could she have stayed in all of this time without me seeing her?"

He repeated, "She was always in there."

"Cows can open latches but they can't shut them behind themselves," I said.

I returned to the carriage house to witness the chicken coop being reinforced against the inevitable eventuality of an unarmed, or should I say unwinged, escape and looked out of the window. On the far hillside I saw the forward advance of a great line of sheep, marching single file on the diagonal up the hilltop, the farthest corner where my woodlot meets the pasture, at the juncture of a lovely old apple tree still boasting of a score or more of yellow apples and a red-berry-covered barberry bush. Between the tree and the bush, visually obscured by the latter, was a break in the wall. The line fence. Easily breached.

"Come on," I said, or rather shouted from the carriage house window with all of the newly found power from being able to breathe once more. The lead sheep stopped and looked toward me. The others, immediately behind, turned their heads and stopped, unanimous in indecision. The rear guard approached, single file, narrowing the ranks. And then, as one, they turned their faces from me and continued on their way up the hill to the line fence. They knew I was too far away to exert any serious influence on them. Suddenly, the calf appeared to join the end of the procession. Next came my donkey, Giuseppe Patrick Nunzio MacGuire, followed by a red exclamation mark, last in line, none other than Lady Agatha Van der Horn, bred heifer, soon to be first-calf heifer.

I tore down the carriage house steps, raced across the pastures, not even stopping to latch the gates, calling, "Cahm ahn, cahm ahn" as I ran. They didn't even glance in my direction. The calf, donkey, and heifer quickened their pace. Lady Annabella was the only one left behind. I stumbled across the stone bridgeway crossing the brook, and ran up the side hill. They disappeared from view. Ninety-nine sheep, one donkey, one calf, and Lady Agatha Van der Horn. I called my neighbors, the ones with the apples on their lawn. "Seen any sheep?" I asked.

"No," he replied.

"Well, my whole farm has headed your way. Could you please call me when they get there and I'll come and get them? Again."

THE SIMPLE LIFE

THE BIRD, black, still, its red wings tucked neatly to its sides, rested on a branch of Michaelmas daisy. Ivory colored. Starlight in the afternoon. Its weight barely bending the tall stem. Silent. Motionless. I saw it. It heard me. It did not move. I waited. It stayed.

This morning, from the dining room windows, I saw another bird. Dark. Almost black. As large as the red-winged blackbird was small. It sat, quite comfortably, on the massive post supporting the fence around the marsh on the far side of the brook. I walked, with deliberate speed, toward it. Through the gate separating lawn from meadow. Across the pasture. Through still another gate. Across the little bridge. The vulture spread its wings and, slowly airborne, flew away. Soon others came. The air was laden with their massive wings. Beautiful, each one of them, separately and together, one by one finding, each a current on which to glide. Mysterious. Without apparent order. Even more of them covered the ground. Black shapes. Their majesty gone. They are the tidiers of the earth, the forest, the pasture. When they left, not even a drop of blood remained on the ribs of the sheep the coyotes had killed early this morning.

There is no reasonable balance to the life here. Sometimes there is harmony. And sometimes less than that. But rare is a balanced moment. Farming is the most intense thing I have ever done in a most intensely lived life. Sometimes I think I shall never stop crying. And sometimes the silence is so perfect it seems as if it shall last forever. When the day goes well, it holds the most peaceful silence of all, a stillness so absolute it can be touched only by God. And when it does not go well, disquietude fills the corners of the heart and turns the mind to shades of gray.

This is not the simple life. It is even more complex than I who live it can grasp. It includes the tiny insects that run across this page as I write. Nearly invisible were it not for the lamp that shines down on them. Early evening. I kill some of them. I'm not certain what kind of insects they are but know I don't want them here. And yet I somehow cannot touch the one that most tempts my hand, following the ink as it crosses the page.

Wind carrying rain makes sails of the enormous pines around the house. I wait for the coyotes across the valley to begin their evening call. They are silent still. Perhaps nothing shall die tonight. Except the tiny insects that I shall feed to the fluffy yellow baby chick that lives in a coffee can under the lamp on the kitchen table. I am teaching it to hunt. It knows, however, that I am not its mother. It sits reluctantly between my hands, chirping frantically to be released, and yet it will perch with enthusiasm on my shoulder. I bend to encourage it to walk back onto the kitchen table, but it doesn't want to leave the soft flannel of my shirt. This is not the simple life.

THE SWEET TIME

I T IS A raw, nasty, gray, snow-blackened meltdown kind of miserable day that I have chosen to be my day of renewed hope. It is only on this kind of day that hope can truly be renewed, for why should one need even to consider searching for hope on other kinds of days?

A lamb sits in my lap. The nipple from a bottle of milk is in his mouth. He is only beginning to learn to drink from it, having been fed through a stomach tube for the first two days of his life. Lambs are enchanting creatures when new. This little one is destined to become a very big sheep. He is as tall and long and has a far bigger head than a two-week-old twin ram that also is in the kitchen. He is the kind I like the best. Or so I think at the moment. The kind that gives me the most pleasure to look at, square and chunky and curly of fleece. A blocky little thing and looks like a living, breathing, moving, and occasionally bottle-drinking doll. Relaxed and peaceful on my lap, he takes a sip or two from the bottle. He knows I am the source to assuage the empty rattling in the last of his four stomachs and scrambled around my feet as I entered the kitchen this morning. But while he has put his nose into the milk in the cat's dish, he hasn't begun to associate sucking on the bottle with filling his belly. He is a big lamb for his two days on earth, and I don't want to risk tube feeding him again for fear of injuring him should he struggle. What to do?

Still another lamb dances around the kitchen. She is a refined and lovely thing. Her fleece is already long and silky. Her face is finely drawn and beautifully formed. "Exquisite" is a word that could appropriately be applied to her. She, too, has claims on the word "favorite" in my eye. A violet ribbon on her neck designates her stakes in my newest flock. She is the exact opposite of the one now asleep in my lap. Oh, I have said of each, you are perfect.

I slept the entire night last night for the first time in recent memory. I got up very late and went downstairs to find the fire out. The kitchen felt dry, however. The day outside it is raw and gloomy. The melting snow betrays all of the winterlong efforts exerted to try to make the house warm. Black ash is everywhere on the snow, as are the remains of a frozen pumpkin that I had tossed to the geese and a bag of potatoes that had frozen when I mistakenly left them in the living room for a misguided day or two. I meant to toss them to the geese, but before I did they became buried, then embedded in the snow on the back porch. All things conspire to remind me how deficient I can be at managing winter.

But I came downstairs this morning quite without dread. Three of the four tiny kitchen lambs danced for me. A few embers left in the new wood stove caught at the paper and bark pyramid I built in it. The sight of a fire in the stove through the glass doors is an outstanding pleasure. A loaf of bread I was too tired to cut into last night is still in its pan in the oven. There was some coffee left in the pot to heat and have a cup in between feeding the older lambs. They are being weaned over the next two weeks, as they are beyond the age for needing milk replacer. They eat grain and now shall have the very best of my latest hay. Their brothers remain in the pen in the summer kitchen. The littlest are light enough to leap the walls of the beautiful new pen, to race up the stairs to stand by the door when they hear my voice from the kitchen answering the ring of the telephone. She's here. Hooray. Bottles.

The main focus on the farm is shifting to the carriage house. The shift has been gradual. I love it when that happens. The scale of that building is quite different from the others on this farm. And it pleases me so. I brought milk, early morning, to the slowly-being-weaned group of replacement ewe lambs who are now living in one of the horse stalls. The loveliest one, Cordelia, still gets a bottle three times a day. She isn't picking up the way she should and I don't want her to compete with the others for milk. They all get hay. The lambs get a sweet feed, a sort of molasses-laden granola that smells yummy enough for me to wish I could eat. The cow doesn't. And so she puts her enormous brown fuzzy head with the fluffy orange ears over the stall gate trying to reach the grain. The lambs are enchanted with her and run to her, stretching as tall as they can to try to touch Lady Agatha Van der Horn's face. Nothing can delight me more. The two white goats divide their time equally between the barn and the carriage house. I didn't know how to have them disbudded when they were babies, and now their horns make life a little less idyllic than it would be without them. But they are pretty, those two, Celeste Baldwin and her daughter Virginia. They are blocky little things, chunky and strong. They eat a lot and always look as if they are quite pregnant. Celeste is with certainty, but I suspect Virginia lost hers in January. They like to be in the carriage house when I am and come to the kitchen door for water when they grow tired of eating snow. They don't have access to the brook as do the sheep and are dependent on what they can get nearer the house.

There is still an egg eater in the chicken coop. I don't know if it is another chicken or a skunk. It can't be a rat, as the four wild barn cats now live there full-time. Oh, I do see them in the barn on occasion, but it is the carriage house where the main events in their lives take place. Pretty little Perkins still stares at me and purrs from a safe distance, asking for milk. I give her some of the lambs' milk replacer in an old cow waterer. The carriage house cats all come out for milk. They catch their own dinners, thank you very much, and I no longer have holes in the feed bags that fill the center floor of the building. I've been offered help from two quarters with the building and have gratefully accepted it. One person has taken it upon himself to do the carpentry that is necessary there to restore one of the existing horse stalls and hay drops so the goats can winter there well and create some new features that will enable me to better use the space. Soon the goats shall freshen and live there with their kids. The milking stands are already installed. It is my farm in miniature in that building. I shall love it soon again. I think one of the nice things about today is that it stretches unadorned before me. I expect no one. No interruptions besides the normally reoccurring ones. No people to deter me from my attempts to perform my appointed tasks. A possibility that I might live the day correctly or, at least, as I see correctly. "To make something better and nothing worse."

I keep notebooks. Those of this past year have now become too numerous. They are fine notebooks, five subject ones with brown paper dividers containing two pockets each in which to keep things. It became quickly apparent that they needed tables of contents so I'd know what was in them, and so I took to numbering their pages. "Personal: Page 2"; "Where is it?" consisting of a list of things I commonly put in a good safe place, a place that is logical, safe, and self-explanatory until the moment, three or four months later, when I can't remember where the safe place is. My mind is visual. Where I've put something on a day when the view from the window is green and light is hard if not impossible for me to envision in the dead of the winter.

It snows. The temperature has dropped. The kitchen is warm. With great comfort the lambs sleep, one like a rag doll in my lap. It is a Sunday. I am determined to change the tablecloth on Sundays. It can be reversed during the week, but a newly ironed, starched tablecloth should appear at least once in a while. I am determined it shall be on Sunday. I've tube-fed the lamb in my arms once again. His head rests on the crook of my elbow. I long to get up and cut into the loaf of bread still sitting in the oven, but I am reluctant to move the lamb. The fire sings. I am grateful for the new stove. It is the sweetest time of day.

ABUNDANCE

THERE IS still another most beautiful of all lambs here on my lap. The lambs of the past few days have had the large-headed, blocky Dorset look that I need, or at the moment think I need, as does this fine little creature. And Fancy Bewling, which just became her name, has a thick curly fleece and great charm.

There is a long list of names in the section of my workbook entitled "farm." I've chosen approximately twelve, to date, for the thirty lambs in the carriage house, summer kitchen, and house. Only one of the barn lambs is named of yet. They are tending to blend in with one another, at the moment, that is. However, they are beginning to be distinguished by braided yarn necklaces and shall all be named soon. Twenty-six of the last names on the list are from the phone book. All versions of Mc or Mac with a few Fitzes thrown in for good measure. They would seem to be a Scottish flock. I tried to name the new East Friesian Whilimena but it didn't take. Whilimena Fitzwilliam. She has become, and it does suit her far better, Phillida Greenleaf. The Greenleaf is after her father, William Greenleaf Sire, now dead. Still mourned. Mariposa Fitzgerald, twins Philipa and Phoebe Turnbottom, Victoria Gainsborough, Cordelia Fitzpatrick and her twin Carlotta (who lives in the barn), and Diedre McCormack are all named. Satisfactorily, I might add. But some of my better names, such as Marvey Chapman and Candida Lycett Green have not found the right lamb to bear their designation. They are too good not to use, however, and among the substantial number to be retained and the eight dairy ewes I am buying in July there shall soon be enough sheep to wear them all.

With the exception of a well-waxed floor, which shall manifest by afternoon, my studio is at last ready for me to work more comfortably. It isn't possible to explain to workmen why an unfinished job can be so disastrous to my life. And so, when a lamp was left only partially rewired, its shade, its huge shade, I might add, placed on my recently acquired highboy, and the rest of its works all over my writing table, I was much hindered from using the room to its proper advantage. For three weeks. It is now repaired and the room is only an hour away from being perfect.

I have bought everything (from a rather modest wish list) in the past four or five months that I care to buy. Books. Books. Books. Garnet velvet for winter curtains in the dining room, a tomato red telephone on which to make calls about the book (which, incidentally, paid for the phone), a beautifully made copy of an old French clock to help keep me working a set number of hours. I've bought five or six more woolen blankets from the Salvation Army. I collect them with a passion. And hay. Hay. Hay. That is it. It is now of interest to me to begin to repair some things. The socket in the lamp in the studio, as an example. And some broken Royal Copenhagen dishes I bought when I first came here. They were too beautiful to throw away. If I am careful with the repair, the single crack in each will be barely noticeable when they are displayed on the long shelf in the kitchen. My copper teakettle requires resoldering, as does a silver plate hot-water bottle I received as a gift a long time ago. It received a dent on its seam when it fell through the then-open grate between the studio on the second floor and the kitchen. It is a good time now to lay out some of the winter blankets while there is still snow to clean them and a warm fire to dry them near. And my collection, again from the Salvation Army, of four-dollar Pendelton wool shirts is due for a hand wash and dry on wooden hangers behind the wood stove.

I've adopted, once again after long disuse, a routine in which to do housework that allows for frequent excursions to lambs, now in no fewer than four places in three buildings, sheep in only two places, as well as cow, chickens, goats, et cetera. In fact the routine interrupts itself, but on such a regular basis that it hurries me along, rushing madly to beat the clock.

The carriage house lambs are doing well. I sat with them yesterday, for a while, in the afternoon, braiding tassels to attach to the violet I-am-to-stay necklaces that they so proudly wear. The better to remember and use their names. They prefer to be closer to eye level with me, I've noticed. Sheep as well as lambs. Some came to be petted who never raise up their faces to me when I am outside of their pen. I took a bag of yarn and some scissors and sat down in the middle of them. The black ram lambs, who are now Spencer and Thurgood Churchill (Randolph didn't make the cut), are in there also. As well as a fine, very fine, East Friesian cross ram lamb who is for sale as breeding stock. It would be so nice to make ribbons for the black twin lambs as well, but that feels as if I'm going a bit over the top.

Mrs. Hudson has been in my thoughts a great deal of late. The housekeeper of Sherlock Holmes. I'm having the most wonderful time with the series of Mary Russell-Sherlock Holmes books written by Laurie King. "Mrs. Hudson, I'm home," shouts Holmes. The smell of beeswax furniture polish and freshly baked scones, Mary will observe, indicates he was expected.

The scones are what are getting to me. And the memory of the kind of hot baths I've been, on the occasion of having thawed pipes, able to indulge in my huge claw-foot tub, the kind that Russell also indulges in. And so I tried to bake scones on the top of my new wood stove. The first batch was a moderate success. I used the bottom of a quiche pan, well floured, directly on the griddle. I cut wedges of a round of buttermilk scone dough, firmly laced with some prunes which had been marinated in red wine, opened the damper, first mistake, and put on three very nice triangles of dough under a nicely rounded copper pot I bought a long time ago in France. The bottoms of the scones entertained the idea of burning. They scorched. Slightly. I turned them over onto the floured quiche pan bottom and cooked them a trifle too long again. However, and there is a very big however here, the steam that rose from them when I split them, the texture, and the aroma were absolutely perfect! Now, I don't know if Mrs. Hudson baked hers inside of the range or on its top. Neither Mrs. nor Mr. Holmes divulged that secret. And I don't know how she brought them from the kitchen to the table, keeping the insides hot enough to steam upon splitting them and thereby melting the butter. Herein lies their ability to enchant. But I do know that these, at least these without the bit of crust that Samantha, dog extraordinaire, was given, were worth the single-word paragraph written by Mary Russell at the onset of *Justice Hall*: "Scones."

I've come close to the beeswaxed furniture look that Mrs. Hudson so lovingly achieved with a commercial product called Future. It makes the five wooden doors in my kitchen and the cupboard gleam with the soft shine that my living room furniture used to have when I could buy beeswax-and-turpentine furniture polish in London. Now that I have neighbors with bees I may try to blend the mix myself. Spring cleaning.

Spring shall be here in a matter of days. The sheep that became stranded in the snow this morning was looking for something green on which to nibble. She is very old. Has lived here for a very long time and considered it a reasonable occupation to head on out to find a bit of grass. I got her back, half lifting, half dragging, to a runoff which divides my pastures, through the mud and onto a bit of very water-covered but semisolid earth. There she found the only green plants, about half an inch high, on which to nibble. The sheep are getting the greenest hay I've fed out this year. It is so very nice that I'm back to feeding it in feeders to reduce waste. Nonetheless, they seem to want fresh green pasture instead.

This day the air positively gleams. The sky is Connecticut blue. It is crystal clear. The outdoor thermometer indicates that a long-overdue January thaw is upon us. In March. Change has come slowly upon me. Sometimes I have had to force change. Demand it. Immediately. Usually during times of disaster. I read once that people in concentration camps had a better chance of survival when they didn't think about what had been left behind. I wonder what then happened upon escape or release. I used that piece of information, on occasion, to guide me through the heartbreak and despair that have often accompanied my effort to build this farm and become, myself, a farmer. Now change is before me once again. And while I make no demands upon myself to adjust to my escape and release from the burdens of banks and mortgages, those changes are happening slowly, quietly, gently, of their own accord.

While this February was the worst I have ever known, and the damage to the farm nearly catastrophic, the damage to me was slight. I had what I needed to live through it. Without being battered. Plenty of books to read in the middle of the night when worry and fear awoke me. Some nice chocolate and crystallized ginger occasionally to add to the pleasure. And the absolute freedom occasioned by my mortgage being paid in full. No disaster was compounded by the threat of losing my home. I become gradually, gently, slowly removed from the brutality that this life has sometimes occasioned. The lambs who survived this winter are so very beautiful. And we shall start anew.

THE LORD'S GREAT PROFETS

THERE ARE days so filled with abundance and goodwill and joy that are in so rare a combination that they are to be treasured. Yesterday was such a day. I've been wanting to build a cart in which to haul manure from my barn for quite some time. In this instance, quite some time means a few years. The cart of my dreams was described in a book called *Farm Conveniences and How to Make Them*, published by O. Judd in 1900 and Lyons Press about one hundred years later. The author, who does not seem to be identified, said it took him several years to work out the principles behind the construction of the cart. It needed balance, strength, and maneuverability. However, upon publication of the nineteenth-century version of written plans, small type, no diagrams, one picture, he believed he had achieved the perfect design. I suspect he was right. I shall, this summer, find out.

The wheels of the cart are to be four feet in diameter. The axle is fixed under the upper side bar, an unusual placement. Presumably this helps the cart to be balanced. The cart itself is eight feet long; therefore only two feet of cart stick out on either side of the wheels. The handles accommodate the length of a set of movable extenders, modifying the design, making them proportionally shorter. As I do not want the extenders, it shall be I who shall have to determine their length. I may take a great risk and change the design to accommodate shorter handles. I've been eyeing a particularly fine set of long handles in Tractor Supply. They are varnished. Long. A chestnut brown. They may become the cart handles of choice. Some other designs I've seen for similar carts include bottom slats that pull out so the manure falls out as it is drawn across the fields. That requires the services of a very well-trained donkey, however, to draw the cart as I pull out the slats. I've failed, to date, to use Nunzio to advantage. So the first cart I am planning to build is to be one pushed by hand.

Nonetheless, the very first hurdle has been to find an axle and wheels. Whenever I am being driven around the countryside, I look for wheels. They are not hard to find but they are hard to come by. There would seem to be many, rusted or painted, leaning as decoration around gateposts or on lawns. As tempting as the thought is to drive up to someone's house to offer to buy the wheels, there never seems to be an accompanying axle. Axles are not in my realm of understanding as yet. I haven't looked at any closely enough to understand how friction doesn't bind them to whatever they are carrying; nonetheless, the ideal combination for me is a set of wheels and the very same axle by which the wheels are accustomed to be borne. Therefore, upon visiting a shepherd in Norwich to buy some Horned Dorset sheep, where I spied in a field some wheels that seemed to be hooked up to an axle, my first question was, "How much would you take for them?" His reply was, "I don't know." I knew how much I had to spend. He didn't know how much he wanted. I left, a Horned Dorset ram and ewe in tow, leaving the wheels and axle behind.

A very short time later we spoke again on the phone, agreeing on a price. The price was reasonable both for him and to me. And so, yesterday, Ernest Westcott came in his blue pickup and off we went. The countryside is so beautiful this time of year. We rode for miles over the curving hills of Delaware and Otsego counties, apple trees in bloom and lilacs waiting for one more warm day to release their fragrance.

Before we arrived, Frank Tiffany had pulled the hay rake out of his junk pile. The assembly was exactly what I wanted. However, it needed to be dismantled to be put in the truck to transport home. This was utterly beyond me. Ernest and Frank dismantled the wheels from the rusty axle. Easily. A surprise. Frank said, "It was an all-day job, which took a few minutes."

I had planned to do both my weekly grocery and feed mill shopping yesterday, as well. There could not possibly be room enough in the pickup for everything. I decided that we'd take the wheels and leave the axle and a back door that Frank had leaning against a building waiting in hopes of someone falling in love with it before it rotted (I did and bought it) for another time.

We loaded up the wheels onto the pickup and started the circuitous journey home. I was very happy. We managed to get all seven hundred pounds of grain on the truck and enough groceries to feed my family this weekend. We then headed on home.

When I arrived, I found a long, thin package on the front porch window seat. Inside was a plethora of treasures. A very long time ago, a tenant had left behind, they usually leave one treasure, the perfect garden trowel. Wooden handled. Finely balanced, nice in the hand. Eventually the handle fell off, and I was heartbroken. I still kept the handleless trowel, thinking that someday I might find a new one for it. The first thing I unwrapped from the box was a replica of that trowel. New. With years of service before it. I can now transplant some of the many volunteers, seedlings blown in from the perennial garden, in my lawn to more appropriate settings. There are enough for several new gardens.

Next was an engineer's compass. I've wanted one forever. It is designed to hang on a belt, and although it points to magnetic north, it was accompanied by instructions on how to correct it to designate true north. It has always seemed wiser to explore the woods immediately beyond my hilltop with a compass to hand. Now I have one.

In a circular metal box were some exquisite little brass page pointers, paper thin, in the shape of an arrow to use to mark things in books. Or, rather, to indicate where in a book something is. How often have I tried to mark pages with tiny scraps of paper only to find they have fallen out.

I rarely have the opportunity to indulge in the more civilized accoutrements of life. Suddenly the acquisition of these delicate, pretty bronze metal arrows made me feel like a rich woman wrapped in abundance. Last but not least, wrapped in beige paper, was a long metal tube. Its color was a metallic tomato red. It was unadorned except for a metal loop on one end. Enclosed was something I've wanted for a very long time. The bucksaw had arrived. At last. Rare have the feelings of abundance, freedom, and independence been so intertwined. The book points. The compass. The trowel. The bucksaw. And the set of wheels. I felt as if I had all in one instant everything I need. Particularly since I found someone to commit to working here eight hours in the vegetable garden to get the ground prepared for seeding. Amazing how little it takes for me to be happy.

I took the bucksaw into the living room where I hung it, still in its tube handle, itself a piece of sculpture, on the door frame next to and complementing perfectly my ancient Liberty chintz curtains, liberally decorated with carnations, one of which matched perfectly the tomato red of the bucksaw's handle. That shall never be misplaced.

Ernest and I off-loaded the wheels and leaned them against my carriage house. I'm certain the weekenders driving by shall think I have put them there for decoration. They certainly are a decoration to my mind. And may in fact be a temporary decoration for my carriage house. I put the compass and its very interesting instructions on the desk in my studio for further examination and, when the groceries were put away, I took the page points upstairs to my window seat and picked up a newly favorite book of Chinese mountain poetry. I've so wanted to mark the pages to be able easily to find the poems I like the best. It was an absolute pleasure to be able to put those points to use.

It has been so very many years since I've had the luxury of even beginning to entertain the idea of having what is needed here to make things manageable. Only in the very beginning of buying this property and way before I ever began to farm did I have the money to provide myself with any of them. Lists were made and prioritized. Duly noted in daybooks or in blue ink on long sheets of foolscap paper. They have gradually been diminished as accomplished. But only in the beginning was that wondrous thing called wherewithal to buy the small things that can make a job manageable rather than a chore. Only now, in very tiny increments, are a few of those things possible. And perhaps a very large thing shall manifest as well. A manure cart.

I was reading a poem about animal husbandry the other day, a poem written about five hundred years ago. It described spreading muck on the pastures. The Lord's Great Profets, it called it. There is only one way life here can be made both possible and manageable. And that is when joy is evident and manifest. And so I shall, when the cart is finished being built, paint on its side, "The Lord's Great Profets." And as I wheel it across the pasture, pulling it off the long-awaited cart with a newly purchased muck rake, I, too, shall experience the joy of having "The Lord's Great Profets" in such manifest abundance.

THE HALF DAY OFF

I'VE BEEN wanting to celebrate my appointed Saturday half day off with the intensity of a nineteenth-century country housemaid who is allowed a once-a-month visit to her mother and brothers and sisters on the moor. I could see, in my mind's eye, all week, how I wanted to spend it with such clarity of possibility that I knew the movie would never play. In reality, that is. I had arranged and rearranged the day in all imaginable combinations. How to ask for a ride from the person who regularly takes me, midweek, to town, that would make sense to him? We never go of a Saturday. How to create work for the young man who was to come for the day to help on the farm that would allow me to leave him unsupervised for a few hours? How to get my chores done early enough in the day to be able to leave? And where was that shirt I had ironed a month ago in anticipation of just such a day off?

But I had made an appointment, in the dead center of the day, two o'clock my time, eleven hers, with my daughter to talk about the menus for my son's wedding reception. We were to "come up with something" and converge in New York to "put it together." I didn't want to put off this telephone meeting any longer.

I had decided, some time ago, that I wanted to take Saturday afternoons for myself. And Sunday. After four o'clock. To write letters. It would seem here on the farm that all of my time is to myself, but nonetheless I've wanted a special designated time. Something to look forward to. There is here a tendency to blend all days together. On this Saturday's afternoon off I wanted, with a passion, to do something I seem to do once a week. But don't experience with the same interest. Go shopping. Oh, I go to the feed store, and Rose and Laurel bookstore, and the Salvation Army, and, of late, Tractor Supply, Hannaford, and always Sweet Indulgence. But what I've really been wanting to do has been to go to the antique store in Colliersville and do a little shopping.

We sheared sheep last weekend. Nancy Meiers, Joachim, and Mikhael. Graciously. It took two days. It went even more smoothly than ever. Each year it becomes better. Some of the lambs have had very long fleeces but are too young to be shorn. We give Ivomec to the sheep, which controls most internal and external parasites. Unfortunately, for the lambs, the keds that are hatched out on their mothers after the Ivomec has run its course all jump onto the unshorn lambs. I decided, since the kill span of the wormer is only about thirty-six hours, to wait a week to worm the lambs. By doing so, anything that had, in the interval, attached itself to their fleeces could be killed at once.

The sheep have been, more or less, kept in the barnyard this spring, waiting for the pasture to warm up and begin to grow. I let them out once or twice a day for water. While they are out, I fill their feeders with grain. Some, who are clever and wise, or have lived with me for a long time, stay behind, knowing what I intend to be doing. Of those, a number are lambs. Unenticed by the water in the brook (they are still nursing) or the quarter inch of grass that is on the pasture, they sit and wait, knowing, or at least I think they are knowing, that the molasses-redolent sweet feed is certain to come.

I've marked, with little red braids, the ewe lambs in the barn who are to stay. Several of them watched me as I threw the sacks of feed off of the platform where my hayloft floor once was. Everyone crowded around the feeders. I opened the gate and the rest of the sheep raced into the barnyard. One of the smaller ewe lambs was knocked over in the process. Again and again. I fought my way through and picked her up. She was limp. I draped her over my arm, climbed the ladder out of the barnyard, and took her inside. It would appear that every one of the keds that had jumped from the shorn sheep had found homes on this lamb's long and silky fleece. She was as infested as I have ever seen in the worst ked infestation on the farm. I sat her down on a white sheet on my lap and proceeded to pull them off of her, dropping them into a can as I did. And counted. To my dismay. After I finished ridding her of every ked I could find, with hope devoid of certainty, the lamb put her chin in the crook of my arm and fell asleep.

After a while, I left her in the house and went out to do one of my favorite chores. Mend fences. The hammer I like best to use outside was missing. So I used a beautifully shaped rock, which fit perfectly in my hand, as it had for some of my more remote ancestors. Since most of the nails chosen by my former foreman to hold the boards to the posts had been rather too short at the onset, my next trip to Tractor Supply shall include buying some longer nails. Much longer nails.

A gate dividing a pasture from the cow path was down as well. I had asked a young man who was fixing fence for me last fall to repair it. He didn't. And came to me to get paid for the afternoon saying all of the work I had requested him to do had been completed. There, next to the broken gate, lying in its entrance, was the hammer. I had been looking for it, needlessly, throughout the barn, when the shearer asked for one to build the form onto which to hang the motor of her equipment. I then remembered having brought it out to the young man, who shall remain unidentified, when he said he couldn't fix the gate because he hadn't brought his hammer with him. To fix fence. He probably had repaired the fence with the same perfectly shaped rock I had been using.

One of the four carrying handles had broken off the portable chicken coop. That had been perfectly and beautifully built long enough ago for it to be reasonably entitled to complain of the need for a modest repair here and there. I used the newly found hammer and put it right again. A little proud of myself at that as I had thought I couldn't repair it myself. But it soon became as sturdy as it had once been. I then proceeded to install some of the indoor chickens in it as well. They showed no reluctance to leave the carriage house. One under each arm. I have hopes that they shall begin to lay eggs in the well-protected nesting box in the portable coop.

I went to the house to check on the lamb. She was hiding behind the wood stove. I shut the door to the living room that Peabody the cat, with her usual competence, had popped open. She prefers to sit on the living room furniture rather than the well-pillowed kitchen rocker unless the fire is blazing in the new wood stove. I went to the studio to receive my daughter's call. She is prompt. Were she not, I had some paperwork to address for the farm. The clock moved past the hour and soon it was two-thirty. I fell asleep in the chair. When I awoke, it was three o'clock. I picked up the telephone receiver. The line was silent. I ran through the house. The door from the kitchen to the living room was wide open. The phone was lying on the floor. Off the hook. The lamb had escaped, momentarily, from the kitchen and knocked it down. I called my daughter. It was almost three-thirty.

All things well on their way to beginning to be arranged for the wedding reception, I went outside, visions of pretty or interesting things to have been discovered in the Colliersville shops floating through my mind. I walked the fences on this side of the brook once more to see what was left to be repaired. One small gate had been a problem, leading to a garden plot. I never had understood the proper way to fix it. Suddenly the remedy for its sagging frame became apparent to me. I lay down on the ground, propped my feet on the gate, and watched the moon standing in a cloudless sky. I then watered the cow, donkey, chickens, goats, and remaining lambs in the carriage house using the recently reinstalled garden hose, long frozen, now relieved of its burden of ice, fed the lambs now ensconced in the barn, bottled the formerly ked-covered lamb in the kitchen. Relieved her of what I hoped were the last two, three, or four of the newly hatched miniature monsters and went upstairs to the summer bedroom. I've been airing out my goose-feather comforters and woolen blankets one or two at a time from one of its windows, quite gratified to discover, in that worthwhile volume *Home Comforts*, substantiation for the habit. Sunlight and wind do have a combined effect on said objects that make the practice practical as well as satisfying. The room was cold and clean smelling from its frequent airings. I decided to move into it tonight and made the bed in white sheets and blanket covers and pillows. I then stuck a pen, some chocolate, and a copy of *The Common Reader* (my favorite catalog) in my pocket and took my dog to the neighbor's to see if his currant bushes survived the winter. They did. I sat down at the road's edge, pulled *The Common Reader* from my pocket, and proceeded to mark off some books to dream about. One was *Mountain Home: The Wilderness Poetry of Ancient China*, fifth through thirteenth centuries. Just my kind of thing. "Come on a whim and gone down the mountain, the whim vanished. Can anyone know who I was?"

I spent the night in the pristine and cold summer bedroom. The nighttime sky from the three windows is lovely.

A NOTE ON THE AUTHOR

Sylvia Jorrín has been a farmer in Delaware County, New York, for the past sixteen years. She is one of two women livestock farmers in the three hundred farms of the New York City Watershed. Over the past decade she has published a weekly column about life on the farm in the *Delaware County Times*.

A NOTE ON THE TYPE

The text of this book is set in Bembo. This type was
first used in 1495 by the Venetian printer Aldus
Manutius for Cardinal Bembo's *De Aetna*, and was
cut for Manutius by Francesco Griffo. It was one of
the types used by Claude Garamond (1480–1561) as
a model for his Romain de L'Université, and so it
was the forerunner of what became standard European
type for the following two centuries. Its modern
form follows the original types and was designed for
Monotype in 1929.

I saw the house, last night, as it was the first time I
came upon it, rising suddenly to view tucked deep within a
valley, high in the foothills of the Catskill Mountains. It took
my breath away. In the moonlight, snow everywhere, covering
its roofs, and the edges blurred, it was much as it was the day I
bought it over twenty years ago.

I had never intended t~~o~~ _____ her. My dear grandfather
farmed dairy _____ e. My grandmother was
a lady, who sp _____ a perfect accent and had a maid
to brush her hair before she married her handsome beloved.
She never allowed any of her five daughters to milk. She was
afraid their hands would become coarse, and they would not
find city husbands. Oh, were you to see my hands today,
what would you say to me?

This is the story of the life here, written as it is being lived.
It is about the rhythm of the days and their attendant nights,
the flow of the seasons and their gifts of joy and sorrow. Above
all, it is the story of all of us, my flock, my beloved dogs,
the marmalade barn cats, the cows, goats, chickens, geese, pigs,
and Guiseppe Nunzio Patrick MacGuire, the donkey.
We have together created something far more than any
of us could alone. This is our story.

ISBN 0-965-50178-7

www.sylviasfarm.com

JACKET DESIGN BY JULIE METZ
JACKET PHOTO BY CHRIS LOPEZ

Printed in the U.S.A.

9 780965 501781

1171043